LIMITS OF LIBERTY:

Studies of Mill's *On Liberty*

LIMITS OF LIBERTY:

WADSWORTH STUDIES IN
PHILOSOPHICAL CRITICISM
Alexander Sesonske, General Editor

HUMAN UNDERSTANDING:
Studies in the Philosophy of David Hume

META-*MEDITATIONS*:
Studies in Descartes

PLATO'S *MENO*:
Text and Criticism

PLATO'S *REPUBLIC*:
Interpretation and Criticism

LIMITS OF LIBERTY:
Studies of Mill's *On Liberty*

ARISTOTLE'S *ETHICS*:
Issues and Interpretations

LIMITS OF LIBERTY:

Studies of Mill's *On Liberty*

edited by
Peter Radcliff
SAN FRANCISCO STATE COLLEGE

Wadsworth Publishing Company, Inc.
BELMONT, CALIFORNIA

89557

Third printing: July 1969

WADSWORTH STUDIES IN PHILOSOPHICAL CRITICISM

The idea of a series of Studies in Philosophical Criticism developed in response to a growing problem in American universities. Philosophy can be taught most successfully in small classes; philosophical understanding grows in the course of a dialogue where problems are discussed from diverse points of view by men who differ in experience and temperament. But with the increase in college enrollments, the size of introductory classes has grown larger and the possibility of a dialogue between professor and students more remote. Our hope is that the Studies in Philosophical Criticism will make a dialogue of sorts possible in a class of a hundred, or a thousand, as well as in smaller classes and seminars. Each volume in the series contains a collection of critical writings related to a single classical philosophical text, such as Descartes' *Meditations* or Plato's *Republic*. These critical writings are not substitutes for the classical work, but supplements to it. They should be read in conjunction with the classical text. So used, they will bring to bear on the problems raised by Descartes, Hume, or Plato that diversity of voices and viewpoints which is the heart of the dialogue— and also, we hope, will prompt the student to add his voice to the discussion.

In selecting material for the volumes in the series, the editor has not searched primarily for writings which provide a definitive analysis of the classical text, but has rather selected those papers they thought might be most useful in undergraduate courses in philosophy, both to provoke students into serious engagement with the text and the problems found there, and to present them with a variety of philosophical styles and idioms. Most of the writings reprinted are quite contemporary; they were selected not only for their excellence but also as an indication that many of the classical problems of philosophy persist as centers of current controversy. It is believed that this format also achieves one prime desideratum: it acquaints the student with both the great works of the philosophical tradition and the most contemporary concepts, techniques, and modes of thought.

CONTENTS

Contents

INTRODUCTION

This book of critical studies of John Stuart Mill's essay is intended to aid the reader of *On Liberty* in obtaining a better grasp of the essay and the difficulties that it poses. The number of inexpensive editions of *On Liberty* testify to its continuing general appeal. The present popularity of the essay is undoubtedly partly due to coercion in the major area in which Mill admitted coercion could be legitimately exercised for a person's own good—education. As a major work by an important and extremely influential nineteenth-century English thinker presenting, in vigorous fashion, what is now taken as a classic statement of the liberal position on free discussion and individual liberty, *On Liberty* is often required reading in various philosophy courses, political theory, intellectual history, and an occasional English course. However, Mill's essay deserves its wide reading not primarily because it presents a position of historical interest but because the position presented is still relevant. When Willmoore Kendall, a contributor to this volume and one of Mill's severest present-day critics, writes, "We are still dealing, then, with Mill's issue; and we shall think more clearly about it, I believe, if we keep it stated as much as possible in his terms—" he is not using the familiar gambit of attacking an early defender of a position, thus suggesting that the position has not been improved since 1859; nor is it just an expression of a natural conservative inclination to regard old ideas, even the wrong ones, as better than new ones. Primarily, it shows an apt awareness of the extent to which Mill's issue, the proper limits of legal and social coercion, is still with us. Current thinkers dealing with matters as diverse as homosexual relations between consenting adults, communist speakers on campus, the free dissemination of birth-control information, and the legalization of marijuana have often kept the discussion within Mill's terms. Not only have the terms been Mill's, often the suggested solution has been extremely close to Mill's. The Wolfenden Committee in England, in considering the proper function of law with regard to homosexual relations and prostitution, drew the limits of law in a manner reminiscent of Mill.

There remains one additional counter-argument which we believe to be decisive, namely, the importance which society and the law ought to give

1

to individual freedom of choice and action in matters of private morality. Unless a deliberate attempt is to be made by society, acting through the agency of the law, to equate the sphere of crime with that of sin, there must remain a realm of private morality and immorality which is, in brief and crude terms, not the law's business.

The committee went on to recommend that homosexual relations between consenting adults not be treated as a criminal offense. In the United States, Justice Douglas, in his opinion declaring the Connecticut laws against the free dissemination of birth-control information unconstitutional (*Griswold* v. *State of Connecticut*, 496 U.S. 1964), sought to carve out an area of privacy similar to that defended by Mill: "We deal with a right of privacy older than the Bill of Rights, older than our political parties, older than our school system."

A further reason for the popularity of Mill's essay is that, despite its deserved respect as a classic of unusual contemporary relevance, *On Liberty* is not a formidable work. The ease with which the essay can be criticized, a desirable feature in at least one text in any philosophy course, contributes to its popularity as a text. No serious reader of *On Liberty*, no matter how sympathetic he is to Mill's aims, can read the essay without noting difficulties. *On Liberty* has never had an unqualified defense. Some of the questions raised in any class—e.g., "Are there actions which affect only one individual?"—were raised by Mill's first readers and repeated by most later ones. Because objection is quick and easy, it is important to determine whether such criticism can be sustained. Consequently, more space has been given in this book to expounders and "savers of what is still of value" than to objectors, though they are represented.

Mill divides his essay into five parts: an Introduction; a chapter on liberty of discussion; a chapter in defense of individuality as expressed in various "experiments in living"; and two final chapters, "Of the Limits to the Authority of Society over the Individual" and "Applications," in which Mill gives an extended discussion and elaboration of his basic principles. The arrangement of the papers in this book reflects Mill's arrangement of topics. Albert Levi's "The Value of Freedom: Mill's Liberty (1859–1959)," after setting the essay in historical context, serves as a general introduction by giving a chapter-by-chapter discussion of *On Liberty*. Levi claims that Mill utilizes two distinct defenses of liberty: (1) Mill defends free discussion as a utilitarian, in terms of the good consequences to society; and (2) in defending freedom to choose varying ways of life, he appeals to the values of self-realization.

The next two selections are concerned with the topic of the

second chapter, "Of Liberty of Thought and Discussion." The first, from Alexander Meiklejohn's book *Political Freedom*, is not a study of Mill but an independent discussion of the limits of discussion in terms of the First and Fifth Amendments, the context in which the issue is usually raised in this country. There are important differences between Mill and Meiklejohn. For Mill there should be free discussion not because everyone has a right to his own opinion but because opinions are of value to the public. This is a nonpolitical defense that is not tied to any particular form of government. A ruler persuaded by Mill might well grant such liberty to his subjects. Meiklejohn pushes beyond the First Amendment to offer a theoretical justification of free discussion in terms of democratic political theory.

While Mill and Meiklejohn offer different defenses of free discussion, the results are similar enough so that Kendall's vigorous attack of Mill also applies for the most part to Meiklejohn. Kendall's criticisms, in "The 'Open Society' and Its Fallacies," result from his attempt to describe in some detail what kind of society would result if Mill's principles were put into practice. Kendall holds that among other results the tolerance of all opinions would lead to a relativism destructive of the society.

James Fitzjames Stephen, in his book *Liberty, Equality, Fraternity*, devotes over one hundred pages to a detailed examination and criticism of *On Liberty*. The selections chosen represent a few of his major lines of attack. One set deals with free discussion, but, for the most part, the selections are concerned with the topics of Chapter Three of *On Liberty*. Stephen accuses Mill of confusing individuality with eccentricity and failing to recognize the source of the former. In the final set of selections, Stephen urges that there is nothing wrong with punishing immorality as such through law or by public opinion even if it involves no breach of assignable duties to others.[1] The succeeding selection, from H. L. A. Hart's book *Law, Liberty, and Morality*, is an attack on this contention.

Hart argues only that the law should not enforce morality as such. He is quite willing to grant that Mill erred in making self-

[1] Stephen's thesis, that it is proper for the law to punish immorality as such, has also been urged recently by Justice Devlin—first in his Maccabaean lecture (also discussed by Hart) and then in a series of later addresses, which make frequent reference to both Hart and Mill. Stephen was included rather than Devlin because Stephen's critique of Mill is more broadly conceived and is relatively inaccessible—a matter on which Devlin himself can testify: "I did not then know that the same ground had already been covered by Mr. Justice Stephen in his book *Liberty, Equality, Fraternity* published in 1873. It was not until much later that I was with great difficulty able to obtain from the Holburn Public Library a copy of the book held together with an elastic band."

protection the only ground for interference. The passages where Hart introduces paternalism as another ground for interference, if sound, are as damaging to Mill as any in this book; for Mill abhorred the idea of interference for a person's own good and countenanced with equanimity the almost unrestricted sale of drugs. Despite passages in *On Liberty* which suggest that Mill would maintain that an individual always knows his own interest better than anyone else can, a suggestion to which Hart is unsympathetic, Mill did recognize exceptions to this principle, as the selections from the *Principles of Political Economy* show.

The last four essays in this book are analyses of Mill's leading concepts, principles, and major distinctions. Isaiah Berlin, in a selection taken from his published lecture *Two Concepts of Freedom*, analyzes the concept of freedom used by Mill, contrasting the notion of negative freedom found in Mill with the positive notion of freedom. Benn and Peters argue that Mill's principle "all restraint *qua* restraint is an evil" and his principle that self-protection is the only ground for restraint, if properly interpreted, are formal principles partially defining the moral point of view. Since Mill, despite his claim that these principles have a utilitarian justification, tends to treat them as independent, self-evident principles, it is useful to consider what results when they are so treated.

The most frequent criticism of Mill, common to his critics on both left and right, is that there are no acts without consequences for others. J. C. Rees, in his article "*A Re-reading of Mill's On Liberty*," argues that this criticism rests on a misreading of Mill. Mill is concerned not with acts that have no effect on others but rather with acts that do not affect *certain interests* of others. There is no doubt that this is what Mill meant, but there might be some doubt as to whether, as a utilitarian, it was open to Mill to consider only that type of consequence. In a postscript prepared for this volume, Rees supports his reading by reference to *Utilitarianism* and emphasizes that Mill, despite the repeated reference to acts affecting the interests of others, is interested in a narrower class, actions affecting the rights of others. As Mill notes in the fifth chapter, in competitive situations the actions of one person may affect the interests but not the rights of another and, hence, are not restrained.

The last essay, Marcus Singer's discussion of duties to oneself, instead of defending an area of private morality or immorality, argues that if it is private, it is not a sin. In matters concerning only myself, morality is not involved. I may be foolish in such cases, but I cannot (logically) be bad. Singer gives an account of why he holds the notion of a duty to oneself to be senseless. If what concerns only me is never a matter of duty, there could be no moral grounds for restraining actions of this type.

I have had the opportunity of questioning several people concerning possible selections. For suggestions, always useful though not always followed, I am indebted to Professors A. Sesonske, H. Morris, and R. Weingartner; and to E. Yeghiayan, D. Clark, and G. Dworkin. Mrs. Robert Young's care in typing and preparing the manuscript saved me many hours.

THE VALUE OF FREEDOM:
MILL'S LIBERTY (1859–1959)*

Albert William Levi

✧

I

Exactly a hundred years ago John Stuart Mill published his *On Liberty*. It had been projected as early as four years before when Mill was in Rome in the middle of January 1855, and it is just possible that the first draft was written under the heavy winter Italian sun in Naples and Palermo in the months following. Published at a moment of extreme reaction in the course of Western political history, it is sometimes easy to forget just how contrary was its message to the spirit of the times. Napoleon III was dictator of France. Serfdom still flourished in Russia and slavery in the United States. Most of the Balkans lay under the tyranny of Turkish rule, and in that very Italy in which the treatise was conceived the prisons were filled with men who called themselves partisans of freedom. And yet, so much of the liberal spirit of England in the wake of the first Reform Bill worked in Mill that he thought the political tyranny of autocratic despots had given way to a certain progress in human affairs when political power must henceforth "emanate from the periodical choice of the ruled." It expresses precisely one of those over-optimistic traits which must have made the work a slight anachronism in his time but perfectly at home in our own. Mill's belief that the problem of freedom was one of social tyranny rather than political despotism is a conviction which we a hundred years later may well share, but it is hardly a valid conclusion from an observation of the age in which he lived.

Perhaps it is just this timelessness, this passion for the abstract which Mill owes to Benthamism, which makes the *On Liberty* a statement of liberal principle so radical and at the same time so fundamental that it surely ranks with *The Social Contract* and *The Communist*

* From *Ethics*, XII (1959–60), 37–46. Reprinted by permission of The University of Chicago Press. © 1959 by The University of Chicago. A much shortened version of this paper was originally presented at the twelfth International Congress of Philosophy in Venice in September 1958.

Manifesto as a source for the political and social theory of the Western world. At any rate, it has had a checkered and by no means unambiguous history; and, so marked have been the admirations and antagonisms which it has aroused, that these attitudes which it has provoked are perhaps an excellent diagnostic instrument concerning the political climate of the times. In 1861 it was translated into Russian and became a thorn in the flesh of the Czar's secret police; but fifteen years later another slav, Peter Karageorgevitch, later to become King of Serbia, painstakingly translated it himself into his native tongue. Moreover, prior to the second World War at precisely the moment when Harold Laski and the intellectual leaders of the British Labor Party were appealing to it as a sacred text of political principle, the Japanese Emperor Hirohito, deeming it a potent source of the contagious disease of *kikenshiso* (dangerous thoughts), banished it from the public domain. Source of moral principle, or of contagion, or perhaps both, I shall ask three questions about it in this paper: (1) What is the essence of Mill's position? (2) How in this work does he relate the concepts of freedom and of value? (3) Viewing it now in this centenary of its publication, can one rightly maintain that the main structure of Mill's argument still holds against the economic, political, and philosophical changes of a hundred years?

II

The avowed intention of *On Liberty* is to examine the nature and limits of the power which society can legitimately exercise over the individual, and the reasonable conclusion to which it comes is that the sole end for which this power may rightfully be exercised is the protection of society. But as the argument proceeds, Mill finds it necessary to introduce two subordinate pleas which together really constitute the affirmative core of the entire essay: the first is for complete liberty of thought and discussion within the political order; the second is for the free development of individuality however and wherever it may need to flower. The two pleas seem at first sight to belong to different realms of discourse, for the chief restrictions against the absolute freedom of the intellect in its thought and expression ordinarily come from the political prerogatives of church and state whereas the chief impediment to that free experiment with different modes of life (which both springs from, and is productive of, different forms of character and temperament) is the more informal tyranny of social pressure and the strangling conformity which it seeks to impose. But the political and the social are not finally realms which are so easily separated. The tyranny of the majority may express itself either in the formal structure of legal enactment or in the more subtle social pressures by which society has learned to exercise its mandates. Collective opinion may seek to interfere with individual independence both through civil penalties and through social ostracism and disdain, and that liberty of conscience which in the individual is the source of open and public expressions of opinion is at the same time the motivating power framing the pattern of taste and the structure of the individual life plan. Mill knew well that the same mode of perception which had dictated his much-criticized relations with Mrs. Taylor was also at the root of his equally suspect opinions concerning socialism, the emancipation of women, and British foreign policy. Belief and conduct form one seamless fabric, and the essence of the focal self may show itself in behavior which may be alternatively (and probably in either case artificially) classified as social or political. It appears therefore that political and social freedom are but two sub-classes of a single value universal; if they stand or fall, they must stand or fall together.

Is it the case, then, that this value universal is to be asserted absolutely and without qualification? Attention to Mill's argument shows that this is not the case; all assertions about liberty are to be qualified by reference to two further principles: the principle of rationality and the principle of social utility. The first indicates the area in which all libertarian prescriptions are to be applied; the second is the very justification of the value of liberty itself. Everything which Mill says about liberty is meant to apply to human beings in the maturity of their faculties; for children, primitives, mental defectives, barbarians—all those, in short, incapable of being improved by rational discussion—it has no meaning. And to say, as Mill does, that "liberty, as a principle, has no application to any state of things anterior to the time when mankind have become capable of being improved by free and equal discussion," is to provide a clue to the theory of the civil liberties which, I shall argue, was dearest to Mill's heart, although it could not be explicitly stated because of the old Benthamian lumber never finally cleared away. For Mill's ultimate justification of the civil liberties is that principle of utility which he regarded as the final appeal on all ethical questions. Civil liberties promote the welfare of even that society which attempts blindly to suppress them: they are instrumental in the achievement of the greatest happiness for the greatest number. Thus, curiously enough, even the value of freedom as a prerequisite for the attainment of truth is a relative matter. Mill's passionate partisanship for freedom of thought and discussion, his recognition that truth is one of the fruits of rationality and that the intellect must be free to come to such conclusions as it must, does not explicitly transcend the utilitarian argument. He is, of course, always on the side of the true opinion, but in the name of consistency he must insist that even the truth of an opinion is one of the ingredients in its utility. Thus, in a certain sense there is an implicit conflict between the principle of rationality and the principle of utility which are Mill's guideposts in the application of the libertarian principle.

There is, indeed, a paradox here, and it appears even in Mill's own language. For when he says, "I regard utility as the ultimate appeal on all ethical questions; but it must be utility in the largest sense *grounded on the permanent interests of man as a progressive being*," already pleasure as an end has been qualified by the requirements of the qualitatively human, of growth, and of process. But the essence of the difficulty springs, I think, from the incongruity between Mill's deep-seated sympathy for the purely individual in experience and the highly socialized form of the moral utilitarianism which he had inherited from Bentham. The classical mode of the justification of individual liberty is the doctrine of natural rights. Guaranteed by God, or inherent in the order of Nature, these rights are absolute, inalienable, and self-evident. But Mill specifically abandons a natural rights theory of the civil liberties in favor of the doctrine that they are a public utility. ("It is proper to state that I forgo any advantage which could be derived to my argument from the idea of abstract right, as a thing independent of utility.") And in so doing, in suggesting that the values of freedom are primarily social values, he opens the way for society itself to be the judge of freedom's social utility. But if the judgment of the social value of freedom is left to that type of democratic choice in which the authority resides in a majority of those whose interests are at stake (and it is difficult to interpret Mill's intention in any other way), then just this (ironically enough) is to invite that very tyranny of the majority against which the essay *On Liberty* was specifically directed.

The solution of the paradox is a theory congruent with Mill's basic ideas although not stated explicitly in *On Liberty,* and it would press him further away from the unsympathetic rigor of Benthamism toward the more fluid doctrine of the Idealists or of Dewey. It would be neither a "natural rights" nor a "public utility" but a *self-realizational* theory of the civil liberties. The natural rights doctrine hinges upon a theological foundation which cannot be proved to the satisfaction of a secular age. The social utility doctrine plays into the hands of a possible tyranny of the majority and gives insufficient attention to the absoluteness of liberty as an individual requirement. But the proponent of a self-realizational theory might argue in the following

way. Those same selves which deliberate about the disposition of their
personal lives also must deliberate about questions of social policy. And
just as there must be freedom of self-determination for the inner life,
so there must be freedom for public discussion and deliberation about
outward acts. Selves are largely formed and continually remade in the
process of interacting with their fellows, and the very formation of
responsible selves *requires* that they speak freely, respond to the words
of others, develop the latent powers of their reason by testing the
alternatives before them. For however the self is a social emergent,
growing out of a prior social environment, *selfhood is axiologically
prior to society*, and society must respect individuality in its own
nature as the source of all values. In a certain sense Mill recognized
this. "The worth of a State," he said, "in the long run is the worth of
the individuals composing it." But he did not explicitly state that even
beyond its social utility, the freedom of thought and discussion is *the
very condition of the making of persons*. It is, I think, implied in the
concept of "utility in the largest sense, grounded on the permanent
interests of man as a progressive being"; and if Mill had elaborated it,
such a statement would have passed beyond both a Lockean theory of
natural rights and a Benthamian theory of social utility. And it would
have been a return to Aristotle. For it would have insisted that
freedom is at once a natural right and an absolute requirement but one
which stems from *the natural fact* that only through its enjoyment can
the potentiality of the human animal be actualized, and that only
through its exercise can man attain the perfection of his rational and
his moral powers.

III

It seems clear that Mill's Benthamism commits him to a defense
of freedom of thought and discussion which finds these to be primarily
an instrument in the formation of the public mind and therefore shifts
their justification from the self-determination of the individual to the
self-determination of society. Interference with public discussion in an
attempt to safeguard sacred institutions from attack is intrinsically an
illegitimate power, and even when public opinion is itself at one with
coercive government in this attempt, it cannot be vindicated. And this
because opinion is not merely the possession of its owner, but a public
property instrumental in either affording access to a new truth or
providing for the revivication of an old. The censorship of individual
opinion is therefore in Mill's conception not a private injury but a
public damage. It inhibits the corrigibility of social error, and it puts

an end to that faith in social experimentalism which holds that mistakes within the realm of social policy can be rectified by experience and exposed within the arena of open public discussion. That "steady habit of correcting and completing . . . opinion" is the only guarantee of success in the perfecting of public as it is in the perfecting of private judgment. This is the culminating insight of chapter ii of *On Liberty*.

But it is also clear that Mill's heart lies with the free development of individuality which is itself the condition of all that we understand by society, civilization, and culture, and that in this sympathy is to be found the real clue to the relation between "freedom" and "value" in his system. And this is precisely the burden of chapter iii, "Of Individuality as One of the Elements of Well-Being." The relation of Mill's treatment of the liberty of thought and discussion in chapter ii to his passionate defense of individuality in chapter iii is problematic. On the surface it is a distinction between the inward domain of consciousness and the outward domain of individual self-expression, between the freedom to form new opinions and the freedom to carry them out in one's life, between the need to discover new truths and the need to commence new practices, and perhaps in the orderly outline of the work in Mill's mind this was the original intention. But as one compares the treatment of the two themes in the final draft, it becomes ever more difficult to preserve this specific distinction; and indeed, by a subtle shift of emphasis, the social reference of the two topics becomes almost precisely reversed. In the first place, as Mill himself observes, it is difficult to distinguish sharply between the formation of opinion and its expression or publication. Therefore, in a certain sense freedom of speech is as much a concern of the inner life as is freedom of thought. But even more, the inner freedom of thought is treated from the standpoint of a Benthamite doctrine of utility while the arguments for individuality (though not without Benthamite implications) are couched in intrinsic or absolutist terms. This therefore looks very much like the paradox of an "external" defense of an inner freedom followed by an "internal" defense of an outer freedom. It is certainly true that both defenses are based upon Mill's native sympathy for pluralism—upon the belief that diversity itself is a good and not an evil, that it is "useful" that there should be not only differences of opinion, but also varieties of character and differences in actual experiment with alternative modes of life, and that both of these forms of pluralism are, in effect, a public utility. But in the chapter on individuality this form of proof is minimized and subordinated to that very type of Aristotelian argument or of self-realizational theory which, as I have pointed out, the chapter on freedom of thought and discussion so explicitly lacks. It is the "proper condition of a human being arrived at the maturity of his faculties to use and interpret experience in his own way." And, "The human faculties of perception, judgment, discriminative feeling, mental activity, and even moral preference are exercised only in making a choice." And, "He who chooses his plan for himself employs all his faculties." And finally the famous: "Human nature is not a machine to be built after a model, and set to do exactly the work prescribed for it, but a tree, which requires to grow and develop itself on all sides, according to the tendency of the inward forces which make it a living thing."

The argument is distinctly and unmistakably Aristotelian. The external inducement to such acts as are not congruent with our feelings and our character renders us passive and not energetic. He who exercises deliberate decision employs all those faculties which are specifically human: observation; reasoning and judgment; purposive choice; and, once the choice is made, the firmness of will and self-control to hold fast to the decision. It might be a digest of the relevant portions of the *Nicomachean Ethics*.

Once the self-realizational principle is established, it is possible to turn the argument toward its implementation in a world which constitutes a threat to independence and strength of character. Once it has become clear that "among the works of man which human life is rightly employed in perfecting and beautifying, the first in importance surely is man himself," Mill can state the case against a society which has finally gotten the better of individuality, which exercises over the individual life a hostile and dreaded censorship, which has established as the most respectable of social positions that of those who give unquestioning allegiance to the cult of conformity.

The last half of chapter iii of *On Liberty* is perhaps the most rewarding and the most miraculous to a contemporary audience newly sensitized to the dangers of other-direction and seeing before its very eyes that hatred of peculiarity of taste and eccentricity of conduct which *On Liberty* pointed out in 1859. When Mill goes on, as he clearly does, to recommend examples of non-conformity and eccentricity for their own sakes, it is a great temptation to applaud his courage without at the same time paying marked attention to his aim. But the aim is of the essence of the prescription: it is to combat all of those modern influences which are hostile to pure individuality and to score against that despotism of custom which is a perpetual threat to the self-determination of the independent self.

It is perhaps only if one looks at the outward form of the argument that one can say that for Mill freedom is to be justified by its utility. For clearly, its inner kernel is that freedom is itself the pre-condition for the achievement of all value. Thus a position which on superficial inspection seems to make freedom subordinate to value, upon closer examination makes value subordinate to freedom. In the end this is no paradox. Considerations of both freedom and value are referable to the individual self; and for any self, values are its substantive achievement as freedom is its procedural requirement. Therefore the question of rank is morally irrelevant; freedom and value are mutually implicative. If perceptual objects are for Mill "a permanent possibility of sensations," then valuational objects are for him a permanent possibility of satisfactions, and these values (affective-volitional meanings, as they are) can only be maximized when the individual is free to express his own nature, to construct the pattern of his life, to use and interpret experience in his own way.

It is perhaps finally possible to explain the paradox of the relation between Mill's utilitarian defense of freedom of thought and discussion and his absolute insistence upon the value of individuality in this way. A distinction which begins as one between an inner and an outer realm, between the formation of opinion and the pursuance of a line of conduct hinges in the last analysis upon the form of emphasis employed. In the chapter on thought and discussion this emphasis is upon the pressures which are outwardly and coercively directed upon the formation of opinion. In the chapter on individuality the emphasis lies in the exhortation to the self to maintain itself as a self. The emphases are completely and mutually implicative, for freedom has at least two dimensions or two conditions: external permissiveness and the authentic power of self-directive decision. Chapter ii of *On Liberty* explores the first; chapter iii is primarily devoted to the second. And yet, lurking underneath and thickening the plot of emphasis is another force at work. It is the eternal strife of systems coming to a head in Mill's own personal philosophical development, and it infects *On Liberty* with its utilitarian defense of the civil liberties as it infects the *Utilitarianism* with its qualitative distinction among the pleasures. Both of these great works unfold with an undercurrent of confusion and inconsistency, and it is, I think, because of the quaint circumstance that Mill is at once a Benthamite by ruthless education and an Aristotelian by persuasion and natural election. Much of his most fruitful work is the consequence of this tension, and it would be a task both Procrustean and unrewarding to force the polarities into a format of exact logic. Therefore of the ethical development expressed in the essay *On Liberty* (as of that in the *Utilitarianism*) I think we may rightly say that it is a passionate and embattled Mill breaking from the vestigial wrappings of Benthamite doctrine toward the explicit stand-point of an Aristotelian moral philosophy.

IV

"What then is the rightful limit to the sovereignty of the individual over himself? Where does the authority of society begin? How much of human life should be assigned to individuality, and how much to society?" This is the set of questions with which the fourth section begins, and it emphasizes once again that the central argument of the essay *On Liberty* hinges upon the strategic distinction between that part of individual conduct which has consequences for the welfare of others and which is, hence, amenable to the rightful regulation of society, and that part which, comprising the inward domain of con-sciousness (and including conscience, thought, feeling, opinion, and sentiment in all matters scientific, moral, or theological) is the appro-priate region for the most absolute human freedom. But what kind of questions, indeed, are these that Mill is asking? On the surface it would appear that they are questions of legal jurisdiction to be settled by supplying a *factual proposition*. What is individual is simply that which does not injure the interests of another. What is socially relevant is "any part of a person's conduct [which] affects prejudi-cially the interests of others." In practice it may not always be easy to make the distinction (and Mill both admits the difficulty and in his treatment of "applications" strives heroically to overcome it); but once the distinction *is* made and any individual instance classified, the moral imperative follows automatically. At this level the distinction between the individual and society is a *sociological distinction*, and the problem of freedom is transformed into a problem of applied sociol-ogy. Is this all that Mill is saying? I do not think so.

The boundary between the individual and society is not merely the demarcation of a sociological territory; it is meant also to fix a limit within the domain of values, to inclose also the geography of the spirit. For I do not think it can be doubted that to the more pedestrian sociological distinction between the individual and society Mill adds a dimension of moral idealism. His approving reference to Lord Stanley is revealing, for it shows the form of the moral distinction which has been influential in the formation of his thinking. "All matters relating to thought, opinion, conscience appear to me to be without the sphere of legislation; all pertaining to social act, habit, relation to be within it. . . ." But the first are just the "inward domain of consciousness" which Mill has recognized in his introductory remarks and which, as contrasted with political interaction and social functioning, has a privileged status in the realm of values. This seems to imply that the genuine problem of freedom is meaningful only if we separate the "outer" realm of property relations, power relations, and socially consequential conduct from the sensitiveness and intelligence which constitute the activities of the spirit. The desires of men, their acquisitiveness, their ambition, their social strivings have a right to be treated with *social justice* (and hence are fit objects for political regulation and social control); but only those qualities of moral perception and intellectual capability which go into the formation of attitudes and beliefs have a right to the completest, the most uncontrolled *liberty*. Justice (as Mill was to show in the *Utilitarianism*) is a social virtue, for since it deals with the externals of community behavior, it bears always a determinate relation not merely to the moral norm of equality but to the political facts of legality. Liberty in a sense transcends the realm of the social altogether, although it stands to it almost as the moral a priori stands to the moral facts which it is used to justify and explain. It is like the profound difference expressed in the Bill of Rights of our own Constitution, for while Article I states that "Congress *shall make no law* respecting the establishment of religion, or prohibiting the free exercise thereof; or abridging the freedom of speech, or of the press . . .," Article V states on the contrary that "no person . . . shall be deprived of life, liberty, or property *without due process of law.* . . ." It is the same angle of vision which Mill has appropriated from Lord Stanley for it too presupposes that "all matters relating to thought, opinion, conscience" are "without the sphere of legislation" while "all pertaining to social act, habit, relation" are "within it."

The understanding of Mill's argument in the essay *On Liberty* lies in an appreciation of his dualistic mode of perception, in the distinction between the individual and society at the sociological level, and in the distinction between man's inwardness and his outwardness at the moral level. And surely some of the difficulties and the ambiguities which his critics have pointed out are due to a tendency on Mill's own part to obscure the differences between these two modes of analysis. The fact is, I think, that Mill not infrequently uses the language of social psychology to advance the claims of his moral idealism, and that this practice, so prevalent in chapter iv of the essay, is the precise analogue of using the formal statement of the social utility argument to advance the claims of the civil liberties actually held on self-realizational grounds which we have already encountered in chapter ii.

Be that as it may, Mill's two distinctions, intimately related as they are in his work, have been the target of two lines of powerful criticism, each springing from an essentially monistic point of view. Bosanquet in *The Philosophical Theory of the State* and in the name of his own brand of absolute idealism has challenged Mill's distinction between the inwardness and the outwardness of the moral nature. Dewey in *The Public and Its Problems* and in the name of his own brand of pragmatism has challenged Mill's distinction between the individual and society. But since neither Bosanquet nor Dewey has been at pains to distinguish explicitly the sociological from the moral elements in Mill's argument, the point of the two criticisms is much the same.

It is not possible to reproduce Bosanquet's criticisms in detail, but he notes that for Mill the central life of the individual is something to be carefully fenced off against the impact of hostile social forces, and he finds it unthinkable that individuality, genius, fullness of life, and completeness of development should not be evoked by the play of relations in society, but should rather lie (as he thinks Mill thought it did) in an inner self to be cherished by inclosure and made impervious to those external influences which might damage or corrupt. This denial of Mill's claim concerning the inwardness of the moral nature leads Bosanquet to the further assertion that Mill's demarcation between the individual and the social cannot strictly be maintained. His brief and somewhat inadequate examination of Mill's "applications" in the fields of punishment for irreligion or immorality, the restrictions upon trade, and the institution of marriage are used to further this contention. The heart of Bosanquet's argument is that Mill's discrimination between justified and unjustified social interference in the life of the individual as based upon the supposed distinction between "self" and "others" simply will not hold up; and, true to his monistic presuppositions, he finds Mill's mistakes in social philosophy as illustrated in *On Liberty* to be in the class of those errors "characteristic of all conceptions which proceed by assigning different areas to the several factors of an inseparable whole."

Dewey too denies the antithesis between the individual and the social, but, unlike Bosanquet, it is not in the name of an organicism founded upon an idealistic logic or a holistic aesthetics but in the name of a more adequate social psychology. In his opinion too there can be no isolated and independent individual, but the reasons for this lie ultimately in a genetic account of individual selfhood. Selves are formed in the process of social interaction, they have their genesis in role-taking and linguistic communication, they gain their identity by their identification with primary social institutions. This account has two implications. In the first place, since there are strictly organic conditions which lead men to social relations, no social theory based upon abstractions (such as "individuals" who have "rights" by "nature") can ever be adequate. In the second place, since the relation of individual-society is always mediated by such intervening associations as family, church, professional group, etc., if Dewey had simply maintained that "some primary groupings had claims which the state could not legitimately encroach upon . . ." then the celebrated modern antithesis of the Individual and Society and the problem of their reconciliation would not have arisen. The problem would have taken the form of defining the relationship which non-political groups bear to political union. Dewey does not deny that there are social problems of freedom, but his whole point of view is implicit denial of the terms in which Mill sets the problem.

V

Can the criticisms of Bosanquet and Dewey be sustained? Each has a certain implicit proposal for terminological reform, and perhaps even an alternative format in which to set the issues, and surely this is valuable for the development of social philosophy; but in the end Mill's arguments, I think, are not seriously compromised. Perhaps the best proof of this is that finally both Bosanquet and Dewey are forced to reformulate Mill's distinctions in their own terms. Bosanquet may find uncongenial Mill's distinction between "self" and "other," but he is ultimately forced by the very logic of his own position to admit that "individual mind" is the focal point of the world as experienced, and so in his own formulation the distinction reappears as that between "the individual mind" and "the mind of society." Dewey may find uncongenial Mill's distinction between the Individual and Society, but common sense suggests to him that some human acts have consequences for others, while other human acts affect only the individual immediately concerned, and so in his own work the distinction reappears as that between two forms of social transactions, the public and the private.

We are confronted here with four levels of analysis. The dichotomy of individual-social implies the standpoint of social psychology. The dichotomy of inner-outer implies the standpoint of moral idealism. The dichotomy of individual mind–social mind implies the standpoint of idealistic metaphysics. And the dichotomy of private-public implies the standpoint of political control. Mill, as we have noticed, uses both of the first two, and as I have also pointed out, it is at least understandable that some of the difficulties which his critics have had are due to his inconvenient habit of using a sociological distinction to illuminate a moral claim. On the other hand, it is quite interesting to see Bosanquet transform the problem into one of metaphysics, and it is distinctly valuable to have Dewey turn our attention to the more specific issues of political control.

But whether we address the issue at the level of social psychology, ethics, metaphysics, or political control, Mill is surely right: *at some central core of individuality* a *line of strict demarcation must be drawn*, and it must be maintained with all the resources of political or philosophical power. We may see the problem (as David Riesman has formulated it in the sociological language of our time) as that of maintaining the inner life of the individual against the pressures toward conformity of a large urbanized society. We may see it (in terms which T. V. Smith has learned from the songs of Emily Dickinson) as the protest of the purest privacy against the claim of the solidest institutionalism. Or we may see it (in the wise admonitions of Zachariah Chaffee or Alexander Meiklejohn) as the claim of the civil liberties to absolute respect against the counter-claim of the political state. But "the drawing of the line"—difficult as it may be in practice— is an absolute necessity. It is Mill's peculiar virtue that in the essay *On Liberty* he has stated the problem with a freshness and a moral passion (and also perhaps with a many-sidedness productive of confusion) which is classic, and that he has dramatized "the line of demarcation" in a fashion which attempts to do justice not only to our sociological good sense but also to our ethical intuitions. From him perhaps even more than from Kant or from Jefferson we have become aware that *in the drawing of the line* is the expression of our moral nature because it is our most profound assertion of the *value* of freedom.

FREEDOM OF SPEECH*
Alexander Meiklejohn

☼

I

"Congress shall make no law . . . . abridging the freedom of speech . . ."
says the First Amendment to the Constitution. As we turn now to
the interpreting of those words, three preliminary remarks should be
made.

First, let it be noted that, by those words, Congress is not
debarred from all action upon freedom of speech. Legislation which
abridges that freedom is forbidden, but not legislation to enlarge and
enrich it. The freedom of mind which befits the members of a self-
governing society is not a given and fixed part of human nature. It can
be increased and established by learning, by teaching, by the unhin-
dered flow of accurate information, by giving men health and vigor
and security, by bringing them together in activities of communication
and mutual understanding. And the federal legislature is not forbidden
to engage in that positive enterprise of cultivating the general intelligence upon which the success of self-government so obviously depends. On the contrary, in that positive field the Congress of the
United States has a heavy and basic responsibility to promote the
freedom of speech.

And second, no one who reads with care the text of the First
Amendment can fail to be startled by its absoluteness. The phrase,
"Congress shall make no law . . . abridging the freedom of speech," is
unqualified. It admits of no exceptions. To say that no laws of a given
type shall be made means that no laws of that type shall, under any
circumstances, be made. That prohibition holds good in war as in
peace, in danger as in security. The men who adopted the Bill of
Rights were not ignorant of the necessities of war or of national
danger. It would, in fact, be nearer to the truth to say that it was
exactly those necessities which they had in mind as they planned to

* From *Political Freedom* by Alexander Meiklejohn (New York: Harper &
Brothers), pp. 19–28. Copyright © 1948, 1960, by Harper & Brothers. Reprinted
by permission of Harper & Row, Publishers.

19

defend freedom of discussion against them. Out of their own bitter experience they knew how terror and hatred, how war and strife, can drive men into acts of unreasoning suppression. They planned, therefore, both for the peace which they desired and for the wars which they feared. And in both cases they established an absolute, unqualified prohibition of the abridgment of the freedom of speech. That same requirement, for the same reasons, under the same Constitution, holds good today.

Against what has just been said it will be answered that twentieth-century America does not accept "absolutes" so readily as did the eighteenth century. But to this we must reply that the issue here involved cannot be dealt with by such twentieth-century a priori reasoning. It requires careful examination of the structure and functioning of our political system as a whole to see what part the principle of the freedom of speech plays, here and now, in that system. And when that examination is made, it seems to me clear that for our day and generation, the words of the First Amendment mean literally what they say. And what they say is that under no circumstances shall the freedom of speech be abridged. Whether or not that opinion can be justified is the primary issue with which this argument tries to deal.

But, third, this dictum which we rightly take to express the most vital wisdom which men have won in their striving for political freedom is yet—it must be admitted—strangely paradoxical. No one can doubt that, in any well-governed society, the legislature has both the right and the duty to prohibit certain forms of speech. Libellous assertions may be, and must be, forbidden and punished. So too must slander. Words which incite men to crime are themselves criminal and must be dealt with as such. Sedition and treason may be expressed by speech or writing.[1] And, in those cases, decisive repressive action by the government is imperative for the sake of the general welfare. All these necessities that speech be limited are recognized and provided for under the Constitution. They were not unknown to the writers of the First Amendment. That amendment, then, we may take it for granted, *does not forbid the abridging of speech.* But, at the same time, *it does forbid the abridging of the freedom of speech.* It is to the solving of

---

[1] I shall be grateful if the reader will eliminate from the sentence, "Sedition and treason may be expressed by speech or writing," the words "Sedition and." "Treason" is a genuine word, with an honest and carefully defined procedural meaning. But "sedition," as applied to belief or communication, is, for the most part, a tricky and misleading word. It is used chiefly to suggest that a "treasonable" crime has been committed in an area in which, under the Constitution, no such crime can exist. (Note added 1960.)

that paradox, that apparent self-contradiction, that we are summoned if, as free men, we wish to know what the right of freedom of speech is.

II

As we proceed now to reflect upon the relations of a thinking and speaking individual to the government which guards his freedom, we may do well to turn back for a few moments to the analysis of those relations given by Plato. The Athenian philosopher of the fourth century B.C. was himself caught in our paradox. He saw the connection between self-government and intelligence with a clarity and wisdom and wit which have never been excelled. In his two short dialogues, the *Apology* and the *Crito*, he grapples with the problem which we are facing.

In both dialogues, Plato is considering the right which a government has to demand obedience from its citizens. And in both dialogues, Socrates, a thinker and teacher who had aroused Plato from dogmatic slumber, is the citizen whose relations are discussed. The question is whether or not Socrates is in duty bound to obey the government. In the *Apology* the answer is "No." In the *Crito* the answer is "Yes." Plato is obviously using one of the favorite devices of the teacher. He is seeming to contradict himself. He is thereby demanding of his pupils that they save themselves and him from contradiction by making clear a basic and elusive distinction.

In the *Apology*, Socrates is on trial for his life. The charge against him is that in his teaching he has "corrupted the youth" and has "denied the Gods." On the evidence presented by a kind of un-Athenian Subversive Activities Committee he is found guilty. His judges do not wish to put him to death, but they warn him that, unless he will agree to stop his teaching or to change its tenor, they must order his execution. And to this demand for obedience to a decree abridging his freedom of speech, Socrates replies with a flat and unequivocal declaration of disobedient independence. My teaching, he says, is not, in that sense, under the abridging control of the government. Athens is a free city. No official, no judge, he declares, may tell me what I shall, or shall not, teach or think. He recognizes that the government has the power and the legal right to put him to death. But so far as the content of his teaching is concerned, he claims unqualified independence. "Congress shall make no law abridging the freedom of speech," he seems to be saying. Present-day Americans who wish to understand the meaning, the human intention, expressed by the First Amendment, would do well to read and to ponder again Plato's

Apology, written in Athens twenty-four centuries ago. It may well be argued that if the *Apology* had not been written—by Plato or by someone else—the First Amendment would not have been written. The relation here is one of trunk and branch.

But the argument of the *Crito* seems, at least, to contradict that of the *Apology*. Here Socrates, having been condemned to death, is in prison awaiting the carrying out of the sentence. His friend Crito urges him to escape, to evade the punishment. This he refuses to do. He has no right, he says, to disobey the decision of the government that he must drink the hemlock. That government has legal authority over the life and death of its citizens. Even though it is mistaken, and, therefore, unjust, they must, in this field, conform to its decisions. For Socrates, obedience to the laws which would abridge his life is here quite as imperative as was disobedience to laws which would abridge his belief and the expression of it. In passages of amazing beauty and insight, Socrates explains that duty to Crito. He represents himself as conversing with The Laws of Athens about the compact into which they and he have entered. The Laws, he says, remind him that for seventy years, he has "consented" to them, has accepted from them all the rights and privileges of an Athenian citizen. Will he now, they ask, because his own life is threatened, withdraw his consent, annul the compact? To do that would be a shameful thing, unworthy of a citizen of Athens.

Plato is too great a teacher to formulate for us, or for his more immediate pupils, the distinction which he is here drawing. He demands of us that we make it for ourselves. But that there is a distinction and that the understanding of it is essential for the practice of freedom, he asserts passionately and without equivocation. If the government attempts to limit the freedom of a man's opinions, he tells us, that man, and his fellows with him, has both the right and the duty of disobedience. But if, on the other hand, by regular legal procedure, his life or his property is required of him, he must submit; he must let them go willingly. In one phase of man's activities, the government may exercise control over him. In another phase, it may not. What, then, are those two phases? Only as we see clearly the distinction between them, Plato is saying, do we know what government by consent of the governed means.

III

The difficulties of the paradox of freedom as applied to speech may perhaps be lessened if we now examine the procedure of the traditional American town meeting. That institution is commonly, and rightly, regarded as a model by which free political procedures may be measured. It is self-government in its simplest, most obvious form.

In the town meeting the people of a community assemble to discuss and to act upon matters of public interest—roads, schools, poorhouses, health, external defense, and the like. Every man is free to come. They meet as political equals. Each has a right and a duty to think his own thoughts, to express them, and to listen to the arguments of others. The basic principle is that the freedom of speech shall be unabridged. And yet the meeting cannot even be opened unless, by common consent, speech is abridged. A chairman or moderator is, or has been, chosen. He "calls the meeting to order." And the hush which follows that call is a clear indication that restrictions upon speech have been set up. The moderator assumes, or arranges, that in the conduct of the business, certain rules of order will be observed. Except as he is overruled by the meeting as a whole, he will enforce those rules. His business on its negative side is to abridge speech. For example, it is usually agreed that no one shall speak unless "recognized by the chair." Also, debaters must confine their remarks to "the question before the house." If one man "has the floor," no one else may interrupt him except as provided by the rules. The meeting has assembled, not primarily to talk, but primarily by means of talking to get business done. And the talking must be regulated and abridged as the doing of the business under actual conditions may require. If a speaker wanders from the point at issue, if he is abusive or in other ways threatens to defeat the purpose of the meeting, he may be and should be declared "out of order." He must then stop speaking, at least in that way. And if he persists in breaking the rules, he may be "denied the floor" or, in the last resort, "thrown out" of the meeting. The town meeting, as it seeks for freedom of public discussion of public problems, would be wholly ineffectual unless speech were thus abridged. It is not a Hyde Park. It is a parliament or congress. It is a group of free and equal men, cooperating in a common enterprise, and using for that enterprise responsible and regulated discussion. It is not a dialectical free-for-all. It is self-government.

These speech-abridging activities of the town meeting indicate what the First Amendment to the Constitution does not forbid. When self-governing men demand freedom of speech they are not saying that every individual has an unalienable right to speak whenever, wherever, however he chooses. They do not declare that any man may talk as he pleases, when he pleases, about what he pleases, about whom he pleases, to whom he pleases. The common sense of any reasonable society would deny the existence of that unqualified right. No one, for example, may, without consent of nurse or doctor, rise up in a sickroom to argue for his principles or his candidate. In the sickroom, that question is not "before the house." The discussion is, therefore, "out of order." To you who now listen to my words, it is allowable to differ with me, but it is not allowable for you to state that difference in words until I have finished my reading. Anyone who would thus irresponsibly interrupt the activities of a lecture, a hospital, a concert hall, a church, a machine shop, a classroom, a football field, or a home, does not thereby exhibit his freedom. Rather, he shows himself to be a boor, a public nuisance, who must be abated, by force if necessary.

What, then, does the First Amendment forbid? Here again the town meeting suggests an answer. That meeting is called to discuss and, on the basis of such discussion, to decide matters of public policy. For example, shall there be a school? Where shall it be located? Who shall teach? What shall be taught? The community has agreed that such questions as these shall be freely discussed and that, when the discussion is ended, decision upon them will be made by vote of the citizens. Now, in that method of political self-government, the point of ultimate interest is not the words of the speakers, but the minds of the hearers. The final aim of the meeting is the voting of wise decisions. The voters, therefore, must be made as wise as possible. The welfare of the community requires that those who decide issues shall understand them. They must know what they are voting about. And this, in turn, requires that so far as time allows, all facts and interests relevant to the problem shall be fully and fairly presented to the meeting. Both facts and interests must be given in such a way that all the alternative lines of action can be wisely measured in relation to one another. As the self-governing community seeks, by the method of voting, to gain wisdom in action, it can find it only in the minds of its individual citizens. If they fail, it fails. That is why freedom of discussion for those minds may not be abridged.

The First Amendment, then, is not the guardian of unregulated talkativeness. It does not require that, on every occasion, every citizen shall take part in public debate. Nor can it even give assurance that everyone shall have opportunity to do so. If, for example, at a town meeting, twenty like-minded citizens have become a "party," and if one of them has read to the meeting an argument which they have all approved, it would be ludicrously out of order for each of the others to insist on reading it again. No competent moderator would tolerate that wasting of the time available for free discussion. What is essential is not that everyone shall speak, but that everything worth saying shall be said. To this end, for example, it may be arranged that each of the known conflicting points of view shall have, and shall be limited to, an assigned share of the time available. But however it be arranged, the vital point, as stated negatively, is that no suggestion of policy shall be denied a hearing because it is on one side of the issue rather than another. And this means that though citizens may, on other grounds, be barred from speaking, they may not be barred because their views are thought to be false or dangerous. No plan of action shall be outlawed because someone in control thinks it unwise, unfair, un-American. No speaker may be declared "out of order" because we disagree with what he intends to say. And the reason for this equality of status in the field of ideas lies deep in the very foundations of the self-governing process. When men govern themselves, it is they—and no one else—who must pass judgment upon unwisdom and unfairness and danger. And that means that unwise ideas must have a hearing as well as wise ones, unfair as well as fair, dangerous as well as safe, un-American as well as American. Just so far as, at any point, the citizens who are to decide an issue are denied acquaintance with information or opinion or doubt or disbelief or criticism which is relevant to that issue, just so far the result must be ill-considered, ill-balanced planning for the general good. *It is that mutilation of the thinking process of the community against which the First Amendment to the Constitution is directed.* The principle of the freedom of speech springs from the necessities of the program of self-government. It is not a Law of Nature or of Reason in the abstract. It is a deduction from the basic American agreement that public issues shall be decided by universal suffrage.

If, then, on any occasion in the United States it is allowable to say that the Constitution is a good document it is equally allowable, in that situation, to say that the Constitution is a bad document. If a public building may be used in which to say, in time of war, that the war is justified, then the same building may be used in which to say that it is not justified. If it be publicly argued that conscription for armed service is moral and necessary, it may likewise be publicly argued that it is immoral and unnecessary. If it may be said that American political institutions are superior to those of England or Russia or Germany, it may, with equal freedom, be said that those of England or Russia or Germany are superior to ours. These conflicting views may be expressed, must be expressed, not because they are valid, but because they are relevant. If they are responsibly entertained by anyone, we, the voters, need to hear them. When a question of policy is "before the house," free men choose to meet it not with their eyes shut, but with their eyes open. To be afraid of ideas, any idea, is to be unfit for self-government. Any such suppression of ideas about the common good, the First Amendment condemns with its absolute disapproval. The freedom of ideas shall not be abridged.

THE "OPEN SOCIETY" AND ITS FALLACIES*

Willmoore Kendall

A little over 100 years ago John Stuart Mill wrote in his essay *On Liberty* that ". . . there ought to exist the fullest liberty of professing and discussing, as a matter of ethical conviction, any doctrine, however immoral it may be considered."[1] The sentence from which this is taken is not *obiter:* Chapter Two of his book is devoted to arguments, putatively philosophical in character, which if they were sound would warrant precisely such a conclusion;[2] we have therefore every reason to assume that Mill meant by the sentence just what it says. The topic of Chapter Two is the entire "communications" process in civilized society ("advanced" society, as Mill puts it);[3] and the question he raises is whether there should be limitations on that process.[4] He treats that problem as the central problem of all civilized societies, the one to which all other problems are subordinate, because of the consequences, good or ill, that a society must bring upon itself according as it adopts this or that solution to it. And he has supreme confidence in the rightness of the solution he offers. Presumably to avoid all possible

---

*From *The American Political Science Review*, LIV (1960), 972–979. Reprinted by permission.

[1] *On Liberty and Considerations on Representative Government*, ed. R. B. McCallum (Oxford, 1946), p. 14 fn.

[2] That is approximately how Mill himself puts it: the words preceding what I have quoted are, "If the arguments of the present chapter are of any validity, . . ." The chapter is entitled "Of the Liberty of Thought and Discussion."

[3] *Cf. ibid.,* p. 9: ". . . we may leave out of consideration those backward states of society in which the race itself may be considered as in its nonage." The distinction seems to turn variously (*ibid.*) on whether "mankind have become capable of being improved by free and equal discussion" and whether they "have attained the capacity of being guided to their own improvement by conviction or persuasion." On the latter point he adds, perhaps a little optimistically: ". . . a period long since reached in all nations with whom we need here concern ourselves." *Cf. ibid.* p. 59, where he refers, astonishingly, to "the present low state of the human mind," that being the point he needs to establish the thesis there in question.

[4] Who should be permitted, in the fashionable jargon of the "communications" literature, "to say what, and to whom."

misunderstanding, he provides several alternative statements of it, each
of which makes his intention abundantly clear, namely, that society
must be so organized as to make that solution its supreme law. "Fullest," that is, absolute freedom of thought and speech, he asserts by
clear implication[5] in the entire argument of the chapter, is not to be
one of several competing goods society is to foster, one that on occasion might reasonably be sacrificed, in part at least, to the preservation
of other goods; *i.e.*, he refuses to recognize any competing good in the
name of which it can be limited. The silencing of dissenters on behalf
of a received doctrine, of an accepted idea—this is an alternative
statement—is *never* justified:[6] it can only do hurt, unwarranted hurt,
alike to the person silenced, to the individual or group that silences, to
the doctrine or idea on behalf of which the silencing is done, and to the
society in the name of which the silencers silence.[7] The quotation I
started with is, then, merely the strongest, the most intransigent, of
several formulations of a general prescription he makes for advanced
societies. We shall do well to examine it, phrase-by-phrase, before
proceeding:

"There ought to exist"—*ought*, so that the prescription is put
forward on ethical grounds—"the fullest liberty"—a liberty, *i.e.*, that
no one (individual, group, government, even society as a whole) is
entitled to interfere with—"of professing and discussing"—that is, of
publicly propagating—"as a matter of ethical conviction"—which,
however, as any reader can quickly satisfy himself by re-examining
Chapter II, is not intended to exclude other types of conviction, "intellectual" conviction for example—"any doctrine"—and "doctrine" is
not intended to exclude, either, since he uses the term synonymously
with "idea" and "opinion"; usually, indeed, he prefers the word

---

[5] Those who regard "absolute" as too strong a term to be deemed a
synonym of "fullest" may wish to be reminded of the following passage (*ibid.*, p.
11): ". . . the appropriate region of human liberty . . . comprises . . . liberty of
conscience in the most comprehensive sense: liberty of thought and feeling;
absolute freedom of opinion and sentiment on all subjects, practical or speculative,
scientific, moral, or theological. [And the] liberty of expressing and publishing
opinions . . . is practically inseparable from [liberty of thought] . . ." (italics
added). And *cf. ibid.*: "No society . . . is completely free in which [these lib-
erties] . . . do not exist *absolute and unqualified*" (italics added).

[6] *Cf. ibid.*, p. 14: ". . . I deny the right of the people to exercise such
coercion, either by themselves or their government. The power itself is illegitimate. The best government has no more title to it than the worst." The statement
could hardly be more sweeping.

[7] Not to speak of "mankind." *Cf. ibid.*, pp. 14–15: ". . . the peculiar evil of
silencing the expression of an opinion is, that it is robbing the human race; . . .
those who dissent from the opinion, still more than those who hold it."

"opinion"—"however immoral it may be considered"—where "immoral" also is used merely to cover what Mill considers the extreme case, the case in which, he supposes, people are least likely to refrain from silencing; and he would be equally willing, as the context shows, to write "however wrong," that is, "however incorrect," "however dangerous," "however foolish," or even "however harmful," and where "it may be considered" is recognizably short-hand for "it may be considered by anyone whomsoever."

It is fashionable, these days, in part because of a fairly recent book by the scientist-philosopher K. R. Popper,[8] to call the kind of society Mill had in mind an "open society"—by at least implied contrast with a "closed" society, that is, an "hermetically sealed" society, in which Mill's grand principle is, by definition, *not* observed. And we are told, variously, by writers whom we may call (because they so call themselves) Liberals, that we have an open society and ought to protect it against the machinations of those who would like to close it; or that we have a closed society and ought, heeding Mill's arguments, to turn it forthwith into an open society; or that democracy, freedom, progress—any or all of them—must stand or fall, according as we maintain or inaugurate or return to an open society; or that all who are opposed to the idea of the open society are authoritarians, enemies of human freedom, totalitarians. We are told all this, however, at least in its application to civilized societies in general (as opposed to the United States in particular),[9] on grounds that have not varied perceptibly since Mill set them down in the *Essay*. We are still dealing, then, with Mill's issue; and we shall think more clearly about it, I believe, if we keep it stated as much as possible in his terms—for no subsequent pleader for the open society has possessed his clarity or vigor of mind—as follows: Ought there to exist in organized society— the United States, *e.g.*—that "fullest liberty of professing and discussing" that Mill argues for? On what theoretical grounds can that liberty be defended? Is openness of the kind Mill's society would possess one of the characteristics of the *good* society? Before attempting to deal

---

[8] K. R. Popper, *The Open Society and Its Enemies* (London, 1945), 2 vols. The term "open society" is of course much older (Bergson uses a distinction between "open" and "closed" society in *Les deux sources de la morale et de la religion*, though for a quite different purpose). Popper wedded the term "open society" to Mill's ideas, and the term "closed society" to those of his *bêtes noires,* Plato especially.

[9] The exception is necessary, because the American arguments are often based on the meaning of the Constitution of the United States, the First Amendment especially.

with these questions, let me pause to clarify certain aspects of his position.

I

First, Mill must not be understood as saying, over-all, something *more* extravagant than he is actually saying. He is fully aware of the necessity for laws against libel and slander, and does not deem them inconsistent with his doctrine.[10] He is aware, also, of organized society's need to protect its younger members against certain forms of expression;[11] which is to say that his "fullest liberty of professing and discussing" is to obtain only among adults. Laws prohibiting, *e.g.*, the circulation of obscene literature amongst school-children, or, *e.g.*, utterance calculated to undermine the morals (however the society chooses to define morals) of a minor, are presumably not proscribed. Nor does the doctrine outlaw sanctions against incitement to crime[12] —provided, one must hasten to add, nothing political is involved (Mill would permit punishment for incitement to, *e.g.*, tyrannicide, only if it could be shown to have resulted in an overt act).[13] And, finally—a topic about which, as it seems to me, there is much confusion amongst commentators on Mill—he would permit the police to disperse a mob where a riot is clearly imminent, even if its shoutings did bear upon some political, social, or economic issue; but not, he makes abundantly clear, on grounds of any official exception to the doctrinal tendency of the shoutings. The individuals concerned would be free to resume their agitation the following morning.[14]

This is an important point because the passage in question, dealing with the mob at the corn-merchant's house, has given Mill an undeserved reputation for having been an adherent of the clear-and-

---

[10] *Cf. op. cit.*, p. 73: "Whenever, in short, there is a definite damage, or a definite risk of [definite?] damage, either to an individual or to the public, the case is taken out of the province of liberty, and placed in that of morality and law."

[11] *Cf. ibid.*, p. 72: ". . . protection against themselves is confessedly due to children and persons under age. . . ."

[12] *Cf. ibid.*, p. 49: ". . . even opinions lose their immunity when the circumstances in which they are expressed are such as to constitute their expression a positive instigation to some mischievous act." To this writer's mind a curious concession, which Mill ought *not* to have made. Once it is made, a society wishing to silence this or that form of persuasive utterance has only to declare the behavior it is calculated to produce a crime, and it may silence—with Mill's blessing.

[13] *Cf. ibid.*, p. 14 fn.

[14] *Cf. ibid.*, p. 49.

present-danger doctrine as we know it today. We may perhaps clear it up best as follows. The situations covered by the clear-and-present-danger doctrine, as applied, *e.g.*, to the Communist "threat," and by parallel doctrines in contemporary political theory,[15] are those in which Mill was *most* concerned to maintain absolute liberty of discussion—those situations, namely, in which the ideas being expressed have a tendency dangerous to the established political, social, or economic order. We must not, then, suppose his society to be one in which anarchists, or defenders of polygamy, for example, could be silenced because of the likelihood of their picking up supporters and, finally, winning the day; since for Mill the likelihood of their picking up supporters is merely a further reason for letting them speak. *All* utterance with a bearing on public policy—political, social, or economic—is to be permitted, no matter what some members of society, even the majority, even all the members save some lonely dissenter,[16] may happen to think of it. Mill must, then, also not be understood as saying something *less* extravagant than he is actually saying.

Second, what is at issue for Mill is not merely unlimited freedom of speech (as just defined) but, as he makes abundantly clear, unlimited freedom of thought as well, *and* a way of life appropriate to their maintenance. To put it otherwise: when we elevate freedom of thought and speech to the position of society's highest good, it ceases to be merely freedom of thought and speech, and becomes—with respect to a great many important matters—the society's ultimate standard of *order*.

Mill did not dwell upon the inescapable implications of this aspect of his position; it has been left to his epigones, especially in the United States, to think the position out. The open society, they tell us repeatedly, *must* see to it that all doctrines start out equal in the marketplace of ideas; for society to assign an advantaged position to these doctrines rather than those would be tantamount to suppressing those; society can, therefore, have no orthodoxy, no public truth, no standard, upon whose validity it is entitled to insist; outside its private homes, its churches, and perhaps its non-public schools, it therefore

---

15 *E.g.*, the doctrine that enemies of liberty must not be permitted to take advantage of "civil liberties" in order to undermine and destroy them; or the doctrine that free society is entitled to interfere with free expression in order to perpetuate its own existence. Mill would certainly not have countenanced either doctrine.

16 *Cf. ibid.*, p. 14: "If all mankind were of one opinion, and only one person were of the contrary opinion, mankind would be no more justified in silencing that one person, than he, if he had the power, would be justified in silencing all mankind."

cannot indoctrinate; *all* questions are for it open questions, and must, publicly, be treated as open. If it has public schools and universities, it will be told (and with unexceptionable logic), these also must treat all questions as open—otherwise what happens to the freedom of thought and so, ultimately, to the freedom of speech of the student who might have thought differently had his teachers not treated some questions as closed? Even if in their hearts and souls all the members of the open society believe in a particular religion, or a particular church, each must nevertheless be careful in his public capacity to treat all religions and churches as equal, to treat dissent, when and as it occurs, as the peer of dogma, to treat the voodoo missionary from Cuba as on an equal plane with an Archbishop of his own church.[17] The open society's first duty (so its custodians will remind it, and if not those at home then those abroad)[18] is to freedom; and that means that it is *not* free to give public status to its beliefs, its standards, and its loyalties. Mill's disciples are completely faithful to the spirit of his thought when they insist that if we mean business about freedom, that is how it is going to have to be. The open society confers "freedom" upon its members; but it does so at the cost of its own freedom as a society.

Third, Mill denies the existence—that is to say, at any particular place and moment—not only of a public truth,[19] but of any truth whatever unless it be the truth of the denial itself. (Let us not press this last too far, however, lest it seem a mere "debater's" point; it is, of course, the Achilles' heel of all skepticisms.) Reduced to its simplest terms, the argument of the *Essay* runs as follows: whenever and wherever men disagree about a teaching, a doctrine, an opinion, an idea, we have no way of knowing which party is correct; the man (or group) who moves to silence a teaching on the ground that it is incorrect attributes to himself a kind of knowledge (Mill says an "infallibility") that no one is ever entitled to claim short of (if then) the very case where the question is sure not to arise—that is, where there is unanimity, and so no temptation to silence to begin with. When, therefore, Mill's followers demand the elevation of skepticism to the status of a national religion, and the remaking of society in that image, they are not reading into his position something that is not there—for all that Mill himself, as I have intimated, preserves a discreet silence on the detailed institutional consequences of his position. They

[17] Who, after all, is to say which is right?

[18] As witness the sermons addressed by the New York press to the Trujillo regime.

[19] Except, we must remind ourselves, the public truth that there is no public truth.

are, rather, only making specific applications of notions that, for Mill, are the point of departure for the entire discussion.

The *basic* position, in fine, is not that society must have no public truth, no orthodoxy, no preferred doctrines, *because* it must have freedom of speech; but that it must not have them *for the same reason* that it must have freedom of speech, namely: because, in any given situation, no supposed truth has any proper claim to special treatment, and this in turn because it may turn out to be incorrect—nay, *will* turn out to be at least partially incorrect, since each competing idea is at most a partial truth. Nor is that all: Mill's freedom of speech doctrine is not merely derivative from a preliminary assault upon truth itself;[20] it is *inseparable from* that assault and cannot, I contend, be defended on any other ground. It is incompatible with religious, or any other, belief.

Fourth, Mill is not saying that no man must be silenced because every man has a "right" to freedom of speech. Consistent skeptic that he is, he warns us—and from an early moment—that he disclaims any advantage that might accrue to his argument from an appeal to abstract right; he is going to justify his position in terms of "utility," in terms of "the permanent interest of a man [*sic*] as a progressive being,"[21] whatever that may mean; and he sticks scrupulously to at least the first half of the promise throughout the *Essay*. This raises interesting questions as to (a) what Mill could have meant—whether indeed he means anything at all that people committed to the idea of abstract right might find intelligible—by such words as "ethical," "immoral," etc.; as to (b) the pains Mill takes, throughout his main argument, to reduce the question, "Should some types of expression be prohibited in civilized society because the ideas they express are wicked?" to the question, "Should some types of expression be prohibited because they are intellectually incorrect?"; and as to (c) the kind of moral fervor his followers have poured into the propagation of his views. Everything reduces itself for Mill to intellectual argument, where you either win or draw or lose by the sheer appeal to reason—which, for Mill, excludes *ex hypothesi* any appeal to revelation or authority, for that would merely precipitate an endless discussion as to the status, from the standpoint of reason, of revelation and authority.

The notion of a "right" to freedom of speech, a capacity on the part of every man to say what he pleases that society must respect, because he is *entitled* to it—of a right that men have to live in the kind

20 *Ibid., passim.*
21 *Ibid.,* p. 9.

of society that Mill projects—is a later development. It occurs in different countries for different reasons and under different auspices; but to the extent that it is intended seriously it represents a complete break with Mill. Those who appeal to such a notion therefore have in his own shrewd example a warning that they must not attempt to do so on his grounds;[22] and much current confusion about the open society would be avoided if they would but take the warning to heart. In short, if we are going to speak of a *right* to freedom of speech, a *right* to live in an open society, we are going to have to justify it with arguments of a different character from Mill's, and so move the discussion onto a plane entirely different from Mill's. We are, above all, going to have to subordinate what we have to say to certain rules of discourse from which Mill, by his own fiat, is happily free. For any such right is inconceivable save as one component of a system or complex of rights, that mutually limit and determine one another and are meaningless save as they are deemed subject to the general proposition that we are not entitled to the exercise of *any* right unless we discharge the duties correlative to that right. Once we begin to argue from premises of that sort we shall begin to talk sense, not nonsense, about freedom of speech and the open society. And the essence of the sense, I hasten to add, will be found to lie in the fact that we are no longer driving the roots of our doctrine into the soil of skepticism, because (as I have suggested already) once we speak of a right[23] we have already ceased to be skeptics. And nothing is more certain than that we shall come out with something quite different from Popper's conception of the open society.

Fifth, Mill was fully aware (as his disciples seem not to be) both of the novelty and of the revolutionary character of his proposal for a society organized around the notion of freedom of speech. Just as he deliberately cuts himself off from any appeal to the notion of abstract right, so does he cut himself off from any appeal to tradition. Not only had no one ever before taught his doctrine concerning freedom of speech. No one had ever taught a doctrine even remotely like his. No one, indeed, had ever discussed such a doctrine even as a matter of speculative fancy.[24] Hardly less than Machiavelli, and more than Hobbes, Mill is in full rebellion against both religion and philosophy,

---

[22] We must distinguish here between a "natural" or "ethical" "right" to freedom of expression and a mere constitutional right. The case for the latter could of course be rested upon Mill's grounds, insofar as they are valid.

[23] Again, we must except the merely constitutional right.

[24] Plato, of course, contemplates a freedom of speech *situation* in Book IX of the *Republic;* but merely to show that it can result only in disaster.

and so in full rebellion also against the traditional society that embodies them.[25] Hardly less than Machiavelli, he conceives himself a "new prince in a new state,"[26] obliged to destroy what has preceded him so that he may create what he feels stirring within him.[27] Hardly less than Machiavelli, again, he is a teacher of *evil:* all truths that have preceded his are (as we have noted in passing above) at most partial truths, and enjoy even that status only because Mill confers it upon them.[28] To reverse a famous phrase, Mill thinks of himself as standing not upon the shoulders of giants but of pygmies. He appeals to no earlier teacher,[29] identifies himself with nothing out of the past; and his doctrine of freedom of speech is, as I have intimated already, the unavoidable logical consequence of the denials from which his thought moves. Not, however, because it is in fact to be the public policy of the society he will found, not because it is to govern his followers' actions with respect to the freedom of thought of others, but because it is the perfect weapon—perfect because of its alleged connection with the quest for truth—to turn upon the traditional society that he must overthrow. For he who would destroy a society must first destroy the public truth it conceives itself as embodying; and Mill's doctrine of freedom of speech, to the extent that it gets itself accepted publicly, does precisely that. I do not, I repeat, believe it can be separated from the evil teaching that underlies it; and nothing could be more astonishing than the incidence of persons amongst us who because of their religious commitments must repudiate the evil teaching, yet continue to embrace the doctrine.

Sixth, Mill's most daring *démarche* in the *Essay* (and Popper's in the *Open Society and Its Enemies*) is that of confronting the reader with a series of false dilemmas: unlimited freedom of speech or all-out thought-control; the open society or the closed society; etc. I say "false" for two reasons: first, because unlimited freedom of speech and the open society are not real alternatives at all, as I hope shortly to show. And second, because the dilemmas as posed conceal the real choices available to us, which are always choices as to how-open-how-closed our society is to be, and thus not choices between two possibilities but choices among an infinite range of possibilities. Mill would have us choose between never silencing and declaring ourselves infal-

---

[25] *Cf.* Leo Strauss, *Thoughts on Machiavelli* (Glencoe, 1958), ch. 4, *passim.*
[26] *Cf. ibid.*, p. 9.
[27] *Cf. ibid.*, ch. 2, *passim.*
[28] *Cf. op. cit.*, pp. 42–46.
[29] That he had broken sharply with his father and with Bentham is, I take it, a commonplace.

lible, as Popper would have us believe that a society cannot be a little bit closed, any more than a woman can be a little bit pregnant. All our knowledge of politics bids us not to fall into that trap. Nobody wants all-out thought-control or the closed society; and nobody has any business pretending that somebody else wants them. For the real question is, how open can a society be and still remain open at all? Or, to put it differently, is there any surer prescription for arriving, willy nilly, in spite of ourselves, at the closed society, than is involved in current pleas for the open society?

II

That brings me to the central business of this article, which I may put as follows. Let us adjourn objections to open society doctrines on the ground that they are rooted in demonstrably evil teachings. Let us also suppose, *arguendo*, that we have organized a society in accordance with Mill's prescriptions, and for Mill's reasons. Have we then cause to suppose, as Mill thinks, that we shall end up forwarding the interests of truth? In other words, Mill offers us not only an exhortation but a prediction, and we wish merely to know what would in fact happen if we did what he tells us to do. My contention will be that, once the question is put in that way,[30] we run up against some insuperable objections to his prescriptions in and of themselves—objections, moreover, that remain equally valid even if one starts out, unlike Mill, from a supposed "right," whether natural or constitutional, to freedom of speech. I shall argue the objections in a logical order such that if each in turn were overcome the remaining ones would still stand.

Mill's proposals have as one of their tacit premises a false conception of the nature of society, and are, therefore, unrealistic on their face. They assume that society is, so to speak, a *debating club* devoted above all to the pursuit of truth, and capable therefore of subordinating itself—and all other considerations, goods, and goals—to that pursuit. Otherwise, the proposals would go no further than to urge upon society the common-sense view that the pursuit of truth is *one* of the goods it ought to cherish (even perhaps that one which it is most likely, in the press of other matters, to fail to make sufficient provision for); that it will neglect this good only at its own peril (a point that could easily be demonstrated); and that, accordingly, it should give hard and careful thought to what kind of provision it can make for it

---

[30] *I.e.*, as a problem for "empirical" political theory.

without disrupting unduly the pursuit of other goods. But we know only too well that society is *not* a debating club—all our experience of society drives the point home—and that, even if it were one, like the UN General Assembly, say, the chances of its adopting the pursuit of truth as its supreme good are negligible. Societies, alike by definition and by the teaching of history, cherish a whole series of goods—among others, their own self-preservation, the *living* of the truth they believe themselves to embody already, and the communication of that truth (pretty much intact, moreover) to future generations, their religion, etc.—which they are not only likely to value as much as or more than the pursuit of truth, but *ought* to value as much as or more than the pursuit of truth, because these are *preconditions* of the pursuit of truth.

To put it a little differently, the proposals misconceive the strategic problem, over against organized society, of those individuals who *do* value the pursuit of truth above all other things. That strategic problem we may state as follows: *fortunate* that society that has even a small handful—a "select minority," in Ortega y Gasset's phrase—of persons who value the pursuit of truth in the way in which Mill imagines a society valuing it. *Fortunate* that select minority in such a society, if it can prevail upon the society to provide it with the leisure and resources with which to engage in the pursuit of truth; or, failing that, at least not to stand in the way of its pursuit of truth. And *wise* that society whose decision-makers see deeply enough into things to provide that select minority—even in the context of guarantees against its abusing its privileges—the leisure and the resources it needs for the pursuit of truth. To ask more than that of society, to ask that it give that select minority freedom to treat publicly all questions as open questions, as open not only for itself in the course of its discharge of its own peculiar function but for everybody, is Utopian in the worst sense of the word; and so, certain to defeat the very purpose the asking is intended to serve. By asking for all, even assuming that all to be desirable, we imperil our chances of getting that little we might have got had we asked only for that little.

If we nevertheless waive that objection, we confront another, namely, that the proposals have as a further tacit premise a false conception of human beings, and how they act in organized society. Concretely, Mill not only assumes that speech (the professing and discussing of any doctrine, however immoral) is incapable of doing hurt in society. (He has to assume this, since he calls for non-interference with speech, while the overriding principle of the *Essay* is that society is always entitled to interfere in order to prevent hurt, whether to itself or to its individual members.) This is disturbing enough: Socrates, we recall, taught otherwise, namely, that he who teaches my neighbor evil does *me* hurt. But Mill also assumes (else again his proposal is romantic) that people can be persuaded either to *be* indifferent toward the possible tendency of what their neighbors are saying, or at least to *act* as if they were indifferent. We know nothing about people, I suggest, that warrants our regarding such an assumption, once it is brought out into the open, as valid. Thus his proposals, like all political proposals that call implicitly for the refashioning of human nature, can be enforced only through some large-scale institutional coercion. And I believe it to be this consideration, above all, that explains the failure of Mill's followers, to date, to persuade any organized society to adopt his proposals. We have no experience of unlimited freedom of speech as Mill defines it, of the open society as Popper defines it, unless, after a fashion and for a brief moment, in Weimar Germany—an experience no organized society will be eager to repeat.

Let us now turn to still another objection. I contend that such a society will become *intolerant*, one in which the pursuit of truth can only come to a halt. Whatever the private convictions of the society's individual members concerning what Plato teaches us to call the important things (that is, the things with which truth is primarily concerned), the society itself is now, by definition, dedicated to a national religion of skepticism, to the suspension of judgment as *the* exercise of judgment *par excellence*. It can, to be sure, tolerate all expression of opinion that is predicated upon its own view of truth; but what is it to do with the man who steps forward to urge an opinion, to conduct an inquiry, *not* predicated on that view? What is it to do with the man who, with every syllable of faith he utters, challenges the very foundations of skeptical society? What can it say to him except, "Sir, you cannot enter into our discussions, because you and we have no common premises from which discussion between us can be initiated?" What can it do, in a word, but silence him, and look on helplessly as within its own bosom the opinions about the important things descend into an ever greater conforming dullness? Nor—unlike traditional society, which did *not* regard all questions as open questions—need it hesitate to silence him. The proposition that all opinions are equally—and hence infinitely—valuable, said to be the unavoidable inference from the proposition that all opinions are equal, is only one—and perhaps the less likely—of two possible inferences, the other being: all opinions are equally—and hence infinitely—*without* value, so what difference does it make if one, particularly one not our own, gets suppressed?[31] This we may fairly call the central paradox of the theory of freedom of speech. In order to practice tolerance on behalf of the pursuit of truth, you have first to value and believe in not merely the pursuit of truth but Truth itself, with all its accumulated riches to date. The all-questions-are-open-questions society cannot do that; it cannot, therefore, practice tolerance towards those who disagree with it. It must persecute—and so, on its very own showing, arrest the pursuit of truth.

I next contend that such a society as Mill prescribed will descend ineluctably into ever-deepening *differences of opinion*, into progressive breakdown of those common premises upon which alone a society can conduct its affairs by discussion, and so into the abandonment of the discussion process and the arbitrament of public questions by violence and civil war. This is the phenomenon—we may call it the dispersal of opinion—to which Rousseau, our greatest modern theorist of the problem, recurred again and again in his writings.[32] The all-questions-are-open-questions society cannot endeavor to arrest it, by giving preferred status to certain opinions and, at the margin, mobilizing itself internally for their defense; for by definition it places a *premium* upon dispersion by inviting irresponsible speculation and irresponsible utterance. As time passes, moreover, the extremes of opinion will—as they did in Weimar—grow further and further apart,

---

[31] *Cf.* Bertrand de Jouvenel, *On Sovereignty* (Chicago, 1957), p. 288: "One of the strangest intellectual illusions of the nineteenth century was the idea that toleration could be ensured by moral relativism. . . . The relativist tells us that the man professing opinion A ought to respect opinion B, because his own opinion A has no more intrinsic value than B. But in that case B has no more than A. Attempts to impose either would be attempts to impose what had no intrinsic value; but also suppression of either would be suppression of what had no intrinsic value. And in that case, there is no crime . . . in the suppression of contrary opinions." On equality of opinions in Mill, see note 16 *supra*. On the progress in Mill from "equally valuable" to "equally and infinitely valuable," *cf. op. cit.*, p. 46: ". . . truth has no chance but in proportion as every side of it, every opinion which embodies any fraction of the truth, not only finds advocates, but is so advocated as to be listened to." And the presumption, he insists, is that every opinion *does* contain some fraction of the truth: ". . . it is always probable that dissentients have something worth hearing . . . and that truth would lose something by their silence" (p. 42).

[32] See *Social Contract*, IV, i., as also *The Discourse on the Sciences and Arts, passim*, and Rousseau's famous letter of 1767 to the Marquis of Mirabeau. *Cf.* de Jouvenel, *op. cit.*, p. 286: "The whole of [Rousseau's] . . . large stock of political wisdom consists in contrasting the dispersion of feelings in a people morally disintegrated by the progress of the 'sciences and arts,' with the natural unity of a people in which dissociation has not occurred." As de Jouvenel notes (p. 287), Rousseau, though himself a Protestant, deplored the introduction of Protestantism into France, and on these grounds.

so that (for the reason noted above) their bearers can less and less tolerate even the thought of one another, still less one another's presence in society. And again the ultimate loser is the pursuit of truth.

Still another tacit premise of the proposals is the extraordinary notion that the discussion process, which correctly understood does indeed forward the pursuit of truth, and does indeed call for *free* discussion, is one and the same thing with Mill's unlimited freedom of speech. They rest, in consequence, upon a false conception of the discussion process. What they will produce is not truth but rather only deafening noise and demoralizing confusion. For the essence of Mill's freedom of speech is the divorce of the right to speak from the duties correlative to the right; the right to speak is a right to speak *ad nauseam*, and with impunity. It is shot through and through with the egalitarian overtones of the French Revolution, which are as different from the measured aristocratic overtones of the pursuit of truth by discussion, as understood by the tradition Mill was attacking, as philosophy is different from phosphorus.

Of the latter point we may sufficiently satisfy ourselves, it seems to me, by recalling how the discussion process works in those situations in which men who are products of the tradition organize themselves for a serious venture in the pursuit of truth—as they do in, say, a branch of scholarship, an academic *discipline*, and the community of truth-seekers corresponding to it.[33]

Such men demonstrably proceed on some such principles as these: (a) The pursuit of truth is indeed forwarded by the exchange of opinions and ideas among many; helpful suggestions do indeed emerge sometimes from surprising quarters; but one does not leap from these facts to the conclusion that helpful suggestions may come from just anybody. (b) The man or woman who wishes to exercise the right to be heard has a logically and temporally prior obligation to *prepare* himself for participation in the exchange, and to prepare himself in the manner defined by the community. Moreover (c), from the moment he begins to participate in the exchange, he must make manifest, by his behavior, his sense of the duty to act as if the other participants had something to teach him—the duty, in a word, to see to it that the exchange goes forward in an atmosphere of courtesy and mutual self-respect. Next (d), the entrant must so behave as to show

---

[33] A similar point might be developed over the difference between Mill's freedom of speech and the free discussion of the traditional American town-meeting.

that he understands that scholarly investigation did not begin with his appearance on the scene, that there is a strong presumption that prior investigators have not labored entirely in vain, and that the community is the custodian of—let us not sidestep the *mot juste*—an *orthodoxy*, no part of which it is going to set lightly to one side. (e) That orthodoxy must be understood as concerning first and foremost the frame of reference within which the exchange of ideas and opinions is to go forward. That frame of reference is, to be sure, subject to change, but this is a matter of meeting the arguments that led originally to its adoption, and meeting them in recognition that the ultimate decision, as to whether or not to change it, lies with the community. (f) The entrant, insofar as he wishes to challenge the orthodoxy, must expect barriers to be placed in his way, and must not be astonished if he is punished, at least in the short term, by what are fashionably called "deprivations"; he must, indeed, recognize that the barriers and the deprivations are a necessary part of the organized procedure by which truth is pursued. (g) Access to the channels of communication that represent the community's central ritual (the learned journals, that is to say) is something that the entrant wins by performing the obligation to produce a craftsmanlike piece of work. (h) The ultimate fate of the entrant who disagrees with the orthodoxy but cannot persuade the community to accept his point of view is, quite simply, isolation within or banishment from the community.

No suggestion is made that this is a complete statement of the rules as we see them operating about us in the scholarly disciplines, or that the particular forms of words employed are the happiest, or most accurate, that could be found. They do, however, seem to me to suggest the broad outlines of the paradigm of the free discussion process as it goes forward in an academic community, and to drive home its differences from the freedom of speech process as Mill defines it. Nor, I think, could anything be more obvious than the answer to the question, which of the two is the more likely to forward the pursuit of truth? But this is not all. *The* point about Mill's model is that by giving equal privileges to those who are in fact opposed to or ignorant of the discussion process, it constitutes a major onslaught against Truth. The two paradigms are not only different, but incompatible.

It would not be easy, of course, to transfer the rules of the discussion process set forth here to the public forum of a society; nor is there any point in denying that the transfer would involve our openly conceding to society far greater powers, particularly as regards silencing the ill-mannered, the ignorant, the irrelevant, than it would ever enjoy under Mill's prescription. Here, however, two things must be kept in mind. First (however reluctant we may be to admit it), that society always has, and constantly exercises, the power to silence. And second, that no society is likely, within the foreseeable future, to remake itself in the image of either of the two paradigms. The question, always, is that of which of the two we accept as the ideal toward which we try to move. That is the real issue at stake between the proponents and opponents of the "open society."

LIBERTY, EQUALITY, FRATERNITY*

James Fitzjames Stephen

[*Moral and legal coercion often for purposes other than self-protection.*]

The application of the principle[1] in question to the moral sanction would be just as subversive of all that people commonly regard as morality. The only moral system which would comply with the principle stated by Mr. Mill would be one capable of being summed up as follows:—'Let every man please himself without hurting his neighbour;' and every moral system which aimed at more than this, either to obtain benefits for society at large other than protection against injury or to do good to the persons affected, would be wrong in principle. This would condemn every existing system of morals. Positive morality is nothing but a body of principles and rules more or less vaguely expressed, and more or less left to be understood, by which certain lines of conduct are forbidden under the penalty of general disapprobation, and that quite irrespectively of self-protection. Mr. Mill himself admits this to a certain extent. In the early part of his fourth chapter he says that a man grossly deficient in the qualities which conduce to his own good is 'necessarily and properly a subject of distaste, or in extreme cases even of contempt,' and he enumerates various inconveniences to which this would expose such a person. He adds, however: 'The inconveniences which are strictly inseparable from the unfavourable judgment of others are the only ones to which a person should ever be subjected for that portion of his conduct and character which concerns his own good, but which does not affect the

---

* From *Liberty, Equality, Fraternity* (New York: Henry Holt and Company, 1882). All page references are to this edition. Original edition published in 1873. The bracketed headings have been added by the editor.

[1] Throughout these selections, unless otherwise noted, when Stephen refers to "the principle" he is referring to the self-protection principle, stated by Mill as follows: "The sole end for which mankind are warranted, individually or collectively, in interfering with the liberty of action of any of their number, is self-protection." [Ed.]

interests of others in their relation with him.' This no doubt weakens the effect of the admission; but be this how it may, the fact still remains that morality is and must be a prohibitive system, one of the main objects of which is to impose upon every one a standard of conduct and of sentiment to which few persons would conform if it were not for the constraint thus put upon them. In nearly every instance the effects of such a system reach far beyond anything that can be described as the purposes of self-protection.

Mr. Mill's system is violated not only by every system of theology which concerns itself with morals and by every known system of positive morality, but by the constitution of human nature itself. There is hardly a habit which men in general regard as good which is not acquired by a series of more or less painful and laborious acts. The condition of human life is such that we must of necessity be restrained and compelled by circumstances in nearly every action of our lives. Why, then, is liberty, defined as Mr. Mill defines it, to be regarded as so precious? What, after all, is done by the legislator or by the person who sets public opinion in motion to control conduct of which he disapproves—or, if the expression is preferred, which he dislikes—which is not done for us all at every instant of our lives by circumstances? The laws which punish murder or theft are substitutes for private vengeance, which, in the absence of law, would punish those crimes more severely, though in a less regular manner. If there were laws which punished incontinence, gluttony, or drunkenness, the same might be said of them. Mr. Mill admits in so many words that there are "inconveniences which are strictly inseparable from the unfavourable judgment of others." What is the distinction in principle between such inconveniences and similar ones organized, defined, and inflicted upon proof that the circumstances which call for their infliction exist? This organization, definition, and procedure make all the difference between the restraints which Mr. Mill would permit and the restraints to which he objects. I cannot see on what the distinction rests. I cannot understand why it must always be wrong to punish habitual drunkenness by fine, imprisonment, or deprivation of civil rights and always be right to punish it by the infliction of those consequences which are 'strictly inseparable from the unfavourable judgment of others.' It may be said that these consequences follow, not because we think them desirable, but in the common order of nature. This answer only suggests the further question, whether nature is in this instance to be regarded as a friend or as an enemy? Every reasonable man would answer that the restraint which the fear of the disapprobation of others imposes on our conduct is the part of the constitution of nature which we could least afford to dispense with. But if this is so, why draw the line where Mr. Mill draws it? Why treat the penal consequences of disapprobation as things to be minimized and restrained within the narrowest limits? What inconvenience, after all, is strictly inseparable from the unfavourable judgment of others? If society at large adopted fully Mr. Mill's theory of liberty, it would be easy to diminish very greatly the inconveniences in question. Strenuously preach and rigorously practise the doctrine that our neighbour's private character is nothing to us and the number of unfavourable judgments formed, and therefore the number of inconveniences inflicted by them, can be reduced as much as we please, and the province of liberty can be enlarged in a corresponding ratio. Does any reasonable man wish for this? Could any one desire gross licentiousness, monstrous extravagance, ridiculous vanity, or the like, to be unnoticed, or, being known, to inflict no inconveniences?

If, however, the restraints on immorality are the main safeguards of society against influences which might be fatal to it, why treat them as if they were bad? Why draw so strongly marked a line between social and legal penalties? Mr. Mill asserts the existence of the distinction in every form of speech. He makes his meaning perfectly clear. Yet from one end of his essay to the other I find no proof and no attempt to give the proper and appropriate proof of it. His doctrine could have been proved if it had been true. It was not proved because it was not true. [pp. 11–15]

[*The exceptions render Mill's principle inapplicable.*]

Not only is an appeal to facts and experience opposed to Mr. Mill's principle, but his essay contains exceptions and qualifications which are really inconsistent with it. He says that his principle 'is meant to apply to human beings only in the maturity of their faculties,' and, he adds, 'we may leave out of account those backward states of society in which the race itself may be considered in its nonage.' Despotism, he says, 'is a legitimate mode of government in dealing with barbarians, provided the end be their improvement, and the means justified by actually effecting that end. Liberty as a principle has no application to any state of things anterior to the time when mankind have become capable of being improved by free and equal discussion. Until then there is nothing for them but implicit obedience to an Akbar or a Charlemagne if they are so fortunate as to find one. But as soon as mankind have attained the capacity of being guided to their own improvement by conviction or persuasion (a period long since reached in all nations with whom we need here concern ourselves), compulsion is no longer admissible as a means to their own good, and is justifiable only for the security of others.'

It seems to me that this qualification either reduces the doctrine qualified to an empty commonplace which no one would care to dispute, or makes an incredible assertion about the state of human society. No one, I suppose, ever denied either in theory or in practice that there is a sphere within which the tastes of people of mature age ought not to be interfered with, and within which differences must be regarded as natural and inevitable—in which better or worse means that which the individual prefers or dislikes. On the other hand, no one ever suggested that it was or could be good for anyone to be compelled to do what he did not like, unless the person compelling was not only stronger but wiser than the person compelled, at all events in reference to the matter to which the compulsion applied.

Either, then, the exception means only that superior wisdom is not in every case a reason why one man should control another—which is a mere commonplace—or else it means that in all the countries which we are accustomed to call civilised the mass of adults are so well acquainted with their own interests and so much disposed to pursue them that no compulsion or restraint put upon any of them by any others for the purpose of promoting their interests can really promote them.

No one can doubt the importance of this assertion, but where is the proof of it? Let us consider how it ought to have and would have been proved if it had been capable of proof. Mr. Mill might have specified the different classes of which some considerable nation—our own, for instance—is composed. Then he might have stated what are the objects which, if attained, would constitute the happiness of each of those classes. Then he might have shown that a knowledge of those interests, a knowledge of the means by which they must be attained, and a disposition to make use of the means proper to obtain them, was so generally diffused among each class that no compulsion put by the other classes upon any one class as a whole, or by any part of any class upon any other part of it, could increase the happiness of the persons compelled to such an extent as to overbalance the pain of the compulsion itself. Before he affirmed that in Western Europe and America the compulsion of adults for their own good is unjustifiable, Mr. Mill ought to have proved that there are among us no considerable differences in point of wisdom, or that if there are, the wiser part of the community does not wish for the welfare of the less wise.

It seems to me quite impossible to stop short of this principle if compulsion in the case of children and 'backward' races is admitted to be justifiable; for, after all, maturity and civilisation are matters of degree. One person may be more mature at fifteen than another at thirty. A nation or a particular part of a nation may make such an advance in the arts of life in half a century that other nations, or other parts of the same nation, which were equally civilised at the beginning of the period, may be relatively barbarous at the end of it.

I do not overlook the qualification contained in the passages quoted above. It fixes the limit up to which compulsion is justifiable at the 'time when mankind have become capable of being improved by free and equal discussion.' This expression may imply that compulsion is always or never justifiable, according to the manner in which it is construed. I am not quite sure that I know what Mr. Mill means by 'equal' discussion, but was there ever a time or place at which no men could be improved on any point by free discussion? The wildest savages, the most immature youths, capable of any sort of education, are capable of being improved by free discussion upon a great variety of subjects. Compulsion, therefore, in their own interests would, at least in relation to these subjects, be unjustifiable as regards them. If boys in a school can be convinced of the importance of industry, you must never punish them for idleness. Such an interpretation of the rule would practically exclude compulsion together.

A narrower interpretation would be as follows. There is a period, now generally reached all over Europe and America, at which discussion takes the place of compulsion, and in which people when they know what is good for them generally do it. When this period is reached, compulsion may be laid aside. To this I should say that no such period has as yet been reached anywhere, and that there is no prospect of its being reached anywhere within any assignable time. [pp. 22–26]

[Confusion of individuality with eccentricity.]

I proceed to the chapter on Individuality as one of the Elements of Well-being.

The substance of the doctrine eloquently expounded in it is that freedom is essential to originality and individuality of character. It consists, however, almost entirely of eulogies upon individuality, to which Mr. Mill thinks the world is indifferent. He accordingly sets forth at length the advantage of having vigorous impulses and plenty of them, of trying experiments in life, of leaving every man of genius free, not indeed 'to seize on the government of the world and make it do his bidding in spite of itself,' but to 'point out the way.' This individuality and energy of character, he thinks, is dying out under various depressing influences. 'The Calvinistic theory' regards 'the crushing out of the human faculties, capacities, and susceptibilities' as 'no evil,' inasmuch as 'man needs no capacity but that of surrendering himself to the will of God, and if he uses any of his faculties for any other purpose but to do that supposed will more effectually he is better without them.' Apart, however, from this, 'society has now fairly got the better of individuality.' All of us are enslaved to custom. 'Energetic characters on any large scale are becoming merely traditional. There is now scarcely any outlet for energy in this country except business.' 'The only unfailing and permanent source of improvement is Liberty, since by it there are as many possible independent centres of improvement as there are individuals.' Individuality, however, is at a discount with us, and we are on the way to a Chinese uniformity.

Much of what I had to say on this subject has been anticipated by an article lately published in 'Fraser's Magazine.'[2] It expands and illustrates with great vigour the following propositions, which appear to me to be unanswerable:—

1. The growth of liberty in the sense of democracy tends to diminish not to increase originality and individuality. 'Make all men equal so far as laws can make them equal, and what does that mean but that each unit is to be rendered hopelessly feeble in presence of an overwhelming majority?' The existence of such a state of society reduces individuals to impotence, and to tell them to be powerful, original, and independent is to mock them. It is like plucking a bird's feathers in order to put it on a level with beasts, and then telling it to fly.

2. 'The hope that people are to be rendered more vigorous by simply removing restrictions seems to be as fallacious as the hope that a bush planted in an open field would naturally develop into a forest tree. It is the intrinsic force which requires strengthening, and it may even happen in some cases that force will produce all the more effect for not being allowed to scatter itself.'

3. Though goodness is various, variety is not in itself good. 'A nation in which everybody was sober would be a happier, better and more progressive, though a less diversified, nation than one of which half the members were sober and the other half habitual drunkards.'

I might borrow many other points from the excellent essay in

---

[2] On 'Social Macadamisation,' by L. S., in *Fraser's Magazine* for August 1872.

question, but I prefer to deal with the matter in my own way, and I will therefore add some remarks in confirmation and illustration of the points for which I am indebted to the writer.

The great defect of Mr. Mill's later writings seems to me to be that he has formed too favourable an estimate of human nature. This displays itself in the chapter now under consideration by the tacit assumption which pervades every part of it that the removal of restraints usually tends to invigorate character. Surely the very opposite of this is the truth. Habitual exertion is the greatest of all invigorators of character, and restraint and coercion in one form or another is the great stimulus to exertion. If you wish to destroy originality and vigour of character, no way to do so is so sure as to put a high level of comfort easily within the reach of moderate and common-place exertion. A life made up of danger, vicissitude and exposure is the sort of life which produces originality and resource. A soldier or sailor on active service lives in an atmosphere of coercion by the elements, by enemies, by disease, by the discipline to which he is subjected. Is he usually a tamer and less original person than a comfortable London shopkeeper or a man with just such an income as enables him to do exactly as he likes? A young man who is educated and so kept under close and continuous discipline till he is twenty-two or twenty-three years of age will generally have a much more vigorous and more original character than one who is left entirely to his own devices at an age when his mind and tastes are unformed. Almost every human being requires more or less coercion and restraint as astringents to give him the maximum of power which he is capable of attaining. The maximum attainable in particular cases depends upon something altogether independent of social arrangements—namely, the nature of the human being himself who is subjected to them; and what this is or how it is to be affected are questions which no one has yet answered. [p. 41]

The odd manner in which Mr. Mill worships mere variety, and confounds the proposition that variety is good with the proposition that goodness is various, is well illustrated by the lines which follow this passage:—'Exceptional individuals . . . should be encouraged in acting differently from the mass'—in order that there may be enough of them to 'point out the way.' Eccentricity is much required in these days. Precisely because the tyranny of opinion is such as to make eccentricity a reproach, it is desirable, in order to break through that tyranny, that people should be eccentric. Eccentricity has always abounded when and where strength of character has abounded, and the amount of eccentricity in a society has generally been proportioned to the amount of genius, mental vigour, and moral courage it contained.

That so few now dare to be eccentric makes the chief danger of the time.

If this advice were followed, we should have as many little oddities in manner and behaviour as we have people who wish to pass for men of genius. Eccentricity is far more often a mark of weakness than a mark of strength. Weakness wishes, as a rule, to attract attention by trifling distinctions, and strength wishes to avoid it. Originality consists in thinking for yourself, not in thinking differently from other people. [pp. 47–48]

[*Mill's treatment of liberty inconsistent with the principle of utility.*]

To me the question whether liberty is a good or a bad thing appears as irrational as the question whether fire is a good or a bad thing? It is both good and bad according to time, place, and circumstance, and a complete answer to the question, In what cases is liberty good and in what cases is it bad? would involve not merely a universal history of mankind, but a complete solution of the problems which such a history would offer. I do not believe that the state of our knowledge is such as to enable us to enunciate any 'very simple principle as entitled to govern absolutely the dealings of society with the individual in the way of compulsion and control.' We must proceed in a far more cautious way, and confine ourselves to such remarks as experience suggests about the advantages and disadvantages of compulsion and liberty respectively in particular cases.

The following way of stating the matter is not and does not pretend to be a solution of the question, In what cases is liberty good? but it will serve to show how the question ought to be discussed when it arises. I do not see how Mr. Mill could deny its correctness consistently with the general principles of the ethical theory which is to a certain extent common to us both.

Compulsion is bad—

1. When the object aimed at is bad.

2. When the object aimed at is good, but the compulsion employed is not calculated to obtain it.

3. When the object aimed at is good, and the compulsion employed is calculated to obtain it, but at too great an expense.

Thus, to compel a man to commit murder is bad, because the object is bad.

To inflict a punishment sufficient to irritate but not sufficient to deter or to destroy for holding particular religious opinions is bad, because such compulsion is not calculated to effect its purpose, assuming it to be good.

To compel people not to trespass by shooting them with spring-guns is bad, because the harm done is out of all proportion to the harm avoided.

If, however, the object aimed at is good, if the compulsion employed such as to attain it, and if the good obtained overbalances the inconvenience of the compulsion itself, I do not understand how, upon utilitarian principles, the compulsion can be bad. I may add that this way of stating the case shows that Mr. Mill's 'simple principle' is really a paradox. It can be justified only by showing as a fact that, self-protection apart, no good object can be attained by any compulsion which is not in itself a greater evil than the absence of the object which the compulsion obtains. [pp. 48–50]

[*Expression of opinions an important matter involving risk.*]

The heretics, says Mr. Mill, are grievously injured by this [social intolerance], and are much to be pitied, but 'the greatest harm is done to those who are not heretics, and whose whole mental development is cramped and their reason cowed by the fear of heresy. Who can compute what the world loses in the multitude of promising intellects combined with timid characters, who dare not follow out any bold, vigorous, independent train of thought lest it should land them in something which would admit of being considered irreligious or immoral?'

On this point I am utterly unable to agree with Mr. Mill. It seems to me that to publish opinions upon morals, politics, and religion is an act as important as any which any man can possibly do; that to attack opinions on which the framework of society rests is a proceeding which both is and ought to be dangerous. I do not say that it ought not to be done in many cases, but it should be done sword in hand, and a man who does it has no more right to be surprised at being fiercely resisted than a soldier who attacks a breach. Mr. Mill's whole charge against social intolerance is that it makes timid people afraid to express unpopular opinions . . . [pp. 77–78]

Till a man has carefully formed his opinions on these subjects, thought them out, assured himself of their value, and decided to take the risk of proclaiming them, the strong probability is that they are not much worth having. Speculation on government, morals, and religion is a matter of vital practical importance, and not mere food for curiosity. Curiosity, no doubt, is generally the motive which leads a man to study them; but till he has formed opinions on them for which he is prepared to fight, there is no hardship in his being compelled by social intolerance to keep them to himself and to those who sympathise with him. [pp. 78–79]

[*The distinction between specific harm and harm to society not useful.*]

. . . there is no principle on which the cases in which Mr. Mill admits the justice of legal punishment can be distinguished from those in which he denies it. The principle is that private vices which are injurious to others may justly be punished, if the injury be specific and the persons injured distinctly assignable, but not otherwise. If the question were as to the possibility in most cases of drawing an indictment against such persons I should agree with him. Criminal law is an extremely rough engine, and must be worked with great caution; but it is one thing to point out a practical difficulty which limits the application of a principle and quite another to refute the principle itself. Mr. Mill's proviso deserves attention in considering the question whether a given act should be punished by law, but he applies it to 'the moral coercion of public opinion,' as well as to legal coercion, and to this the practical difficulty which he points out does not apply. A set of young noblemen of great fortune and hereditary influence, the representatives of ancient names, the natural leaders of the society of large districts, pass their whole time and employ all their means in gross debauchery. Such people are far more injurious to society than common pickpockets, but Mr. Mill says that if any one having the opportunity of making them ashamed of themselves uses it in order to coerce them into decency, he sins against liberty, unless their example does assignable harm to specific people. It might be right to say 'You, the Duke of A, by extravagantly keeping four mistresses—to wit, B and C in London, and D and E in Paris—set an example which induced your friend F to elope with Mrs. G at — on — and you are a great blackguard for your pains, and all the more because you are a duke.' It could never be right to say, 'You, the Duke of A, are scandalously immoral and ought to be made to smart for it, though the law cannot touch you.' The distinction is more likely to be overlooked than to be misunderstood. [pp. 130–131]

[*Law and morality.*]

Society has at its disposal two great instruments by which vice may be prevented and virtue promoted—namely, law and public opinion; and law is either criminal or civil. The use of each of these instruments is subject to certain limits and conditions, and the wisdom of attempting to make men good either by Act of Parliament or by the action of public opinion depends entirely upon the degree in which those limits and conditions are recognized and acted upon.

First, I will take the case of criminal law. What are the conditions under which and the limitations within which it can be applied with success to the object of making men better? In considering this question it must be borne in mind that criminal law is at once by far the most powerful and by far the roughest engine which society can use for any purpose. Its power is shown by the fact that it can and does render crime exceedingly difficult and dangerous. Indeed, in civilized society it absolutely prevents avowed open crime committed with the strong hand, except in cases where crime rises to the magnitude of civil war. Its roughness hardly needs illustration. It strikes so hard that it can be enforced only on the gravest occasions, and with every sort of precaution against abuse or mistake. Before an act can be treated as a crime, it ought to be capable of distinct definition and of specific proof, and it ought also to be of such a nature that it is worth while to prevent it at the risk of inflicting great damage, direct and indirect, upon those who commit it. These conditions are seldom, if ever, fulfilled by mere vices. It would obviously be impossible to indict a man for ingratitude or perfidy. Such charges are too vague for specific discussion and distinct proof on the one side, and disproof on the other. Moreover, the expense of the investigations necessary for the legal punishment of such conduct would be enormous. It would be necessary to go into an infinite number of delicate and subtle inquiries which would tear off all privacy from the lives of a large number of persons. These considerations are, I think, conclusive reasons against treating vice in general as a crime.

The excessive harshness of criminal law is also a circumstance which very greatly narrows the range of its application. It is the *ratio ultima* of the majority against persons whom its application assumes to have renounced the common bonds which connect men together. When a man is subjected to legal punishment, society appeals directly and exclusively to his fears. It renounces the attempt to work upon his affections or feelings. In other words, it puts itself into distinct, harsh, and undisguised opposition to his wishes; and the effect of this will be to make him rebel against the law. The violence of the rebellion will be measured partly by the violence of the passion the indulgence of which is forbidden, and partly by the degree to which the law can count upon an ally in the man's own conscience. A law which enters into a direct contest with a fierce imperious passion, which the person who feels it does not admit to be bad, and which is not directly injurious to others, will generally do more harm than good; and this is perhaps the principal reason why it is impossible to legislate directly against unchastity, unless it takes forms which every one regards as monstrous and horrible. The subject is not one for detailed discussion, but any one who will follow out the reflections which this hint suggests will find that they supply a striking illustration of the limits which the harshness of criminal law imposes upon its range.

If we now look at the different acts which satisfy the conditions specified, it will, I think, be found that criminal law in this country actually is applied to the suppression of vice and so to the promotion of virtue to a very considerable extent; and this I say is right.

The punishment of common crimes, the gross forms of force and fraud, is no doubt ambiguous. It may be justified on the principle of self-protection, and apart from any question as to their moral character. It is not, however, difficult to show that these acts have in fact been forbidden and subjected to punishment not only because they are dangerous to society, and so ought to be prevented, but also for the sake of gratifying the feeling of hatred—call it revenge, resentment, or what you will—which the contemplation of such conduct excites in healthily constituted minds. If this can be shown, it will follow that criminal law is in the nature of a persecution of the grosser forms of vice, and an emphatic assertion of the principle that the feeling of hatred and the desire of vengeance above-mentioned are important elements of human nature which ought in such cases to be satisfied in a regular public and legal manner. [pp. 146–149]

Other illustrations of the fact that English criminal law does recognize morality are to be found in the fact that a considerable number of acts which need not be specified are treated as crimes merely because they are regarded as grossly immoral.

I have already shown in what manner Mr. Mill deals with these topics. It is, I venture to think, utterly unsatisfactory. The impression it makes upon me is that he feels that such acts ought to be punished, and that he is able to reconcile this with his fundamental principles only by subtleties quite unworthy of him. Admit the relation for which I am contending between law and morals, and all becomes perfectly clear. All the acts referred to are unquestionably wicked. Those who do them are ashamed of them. They are all capable of being clearly defined and specifically proved or disproved, and there can be no question at all that legal punishment reduces them to small dimensions, and forces the criminals to carry on their practices with the greatest secrecy and precaution. In other words, the object of their suppression is good, and the means adequate. In practice this is subject to highly important qualifications, of which I will only say here that those who have due regard to the incurable weaknesses of human nature will be very careful how they inflict penalties upon mere vice, if even upon those who make a trade of promoting it, unless special circumstances call for their infliction. It is one thing however to tolerate vice so long as it is inoffensive, and quite another to give it a legal right not only to exist, but to assert itself in the face of the world as an 'experiment in living' as good as another, and entitled to the same protection from law. [pp. 152–153]

I now pass to the manner in which civil law may and does, and as I say properly, promote virtue and prevent vice. This is a subject so wide that I prefer indicating its nature by a few illustrations to attempting to deal with it systematically. It would, however, be easy to show that nearly every branch of civil law assumes the existence of a standard of moral good and evil which the public at large have an interest in maintaining, and in many cases enforcing—a proceeding which is diametrically opposed to Mr. Mill's fundamental principles.

The main subject with which law is conversant is that of rights and duties, and all the commoner and more important rights and duties presuppose some theory of morals. Contracts are one great source of rights and duties. Is there any country in the world the courts of which would enforce a contract which the Legislature regarded as immoral? and is there any country in which there would be much difficulty in specific cases in saying whether the object or the consideration of a contract was or was not immoral? Other rights are of a more general nature, and are liable to be violated by wrongs. Take the case of a man's right to his reputation, which is violated by defamation. How, without the aid of some sort of theory of morals, can it be determined whether the publication of defamatory matter is justifiable or not?

Perhaps the most pointed of all illustrations of the moral character of civil law is to be found in the laws relating to marriage and inheritance. They all proceed upon an essentially moral theory as to the relation of the sexes. Take the case of illegitimate children. A bastard is *filius nullius*—he inherits nothing, he has no claim on his putative father. What is all this except the expression of the strongest possible determination on the part of the Legislature to recognize, maintain, and favour marriage in every possible manner as the foundation of civilized society? It has been plausibly maintained that these laws bear hardly upon bastards, punishing them for the sins of their parents. It is not necessary to my purpose to go into this, though it appears to me that the law is right. I make the remark merely for the sake of showing to what great lengths the law does habitually go for the purpose of maintaining the most important of all moral principles, the principle upon which one great department of it is entirely founded. It is a case in which a good object is promoted by efficient and adequate means. [pp. 153–154]

[*Principles governing interference.*]

Of course there are limits to the possibility of useful interference with morals, either by law or by public opinion; and it is of the highest practical importance that these limits should be carefully observed. The great leading principles on the subject are few and simple, though they cannot be stated with any great precision. It will be enough to mention the following:—

1. Neither legislation nor public opinion ought to be meddle-some. A very large proportion of the matters upon which people wish to interfere with their neighbours are trumpery little things which are of no real importance at all. The busybody and world-betterer who will never let things alone, or trust people to take care of themselves, is a common and a contemptible character. The commonplaces directed against these small creatures are perfectly just, but to try to put them down by denying the connection between law and morals is like shutting all light and air out of a house in order to keep out gnats and blue-bottle flies.

2. Both legislation and public opinion, but especially the latter, are apt to be most mischievous and cruelly unjust if they proceed upon imperfect evidence. To form and express strong opinions about the wickedness of a man whom you do not know, the immorality or impiety of a book you have not read, the merits of a question on which you are uninformed, is to run a great risk of inflicting a great wrong. It is hanging first and trying afterwards, or more frequently not trying at all. This, however, is no argument against hanging after a fair trial.

3. Legislation ought in all cases to be graduated to the existing level of morals in the time and country in which it is employed. You cannot punish anything which public opinion, as expressed in the common practice of society, does not strenuously and unequivocally condemn. To try to do so is a sure way to produce gross hypocrisy and furious reaction. To be able to punish, a moral majority must be overwhelming. Law cannot be better than the nation in which it exists, though it may and can protect an acknowledged moral standard, and may gradually be increased in strictness as the standard rises. We punish, with the utmost severity, practices which in Greece and Rome

went almost uncensured. It is possible that a time may come when it may appear natural and right to punish adultery, seduction, or possibly even fornication, but the prospect is, in the eyes of all reasonable people, indefinitely remote, and it may be doubted whether we are moving in that direction.

4. Legislation and public opinion ought in all cases whatever scrupulously to respect privacy. To define the province of privacy distinctly is impossible, but it can be described in general terms. All the more intimate and delicate relations of life are of such a nature that to submit them to unsympathetic observation, or to observation which is sympathetic in the wrong way, inflicts great pain, and may inflict lasting moral injury. Privacy may be violated not only by the intrusion of a stranger, but by compelling or persuading a person to direct too much attention to his own feelings and to attach too much importance to their analysis. The common usage of language affords a practical test which is almost perfect upon this subject. Conduct which can be described as indecent is always in one way or another a violation of privacy. [pp. 158–160]

PATERNALISM AND THE ENFORCEMENT OF MORALITY*

H. L. A. Hart

THE USE AND ABUSE OF EXAMPLES

Both in England and in America the criminal law still contains rules
which can only be explained as attempts to enforce morality as such:
to suppress practices condemned as immoral by positive morality
though they involve nothing that would ordinarily be thought of as
harm to other persons. Most of the examples come from the sphere of
sexual morals, and in England they include laws against various forms
of homosexual behaviour between males, sodomy between persons of
different sex even if married, bestiality, incest, living on the earnings of
prostitution, keeping a house for prostitution, and also, since the
decision in Shaw's case, a conspiracy to corrupt public morals, interpreted to mean, in substance, leading others (in the opinion of a jury)
"morally astray." To this list some would add further cases: the laws
against abortion, against those forms of bigamy or polygamy which do
not involve deception, against suicide and the practice of euthanasia.
But, as I shall later argue, the treatment of some of these latter as
attempts to enforce morality as such, is a mistake due to the neglect of
certain important distinctions.

In America a glance at the penal statutes of the various states of
the Union reveals something quite astonishing to English eyes. For in
addition to such offences as are punishable under English law, there
seems to be no sexual practice, except "normal" relations between
husband and wife and solitary acts of masturbation, which is not
forbidden by the law of some state. In a very large number of states
adultery, which has not been criminally punishable in England since

* Reprinted from *Law, Liberty, and Morality*, pp. 25–34, by H. L. A. Hart
with the permission of the publishers, Stanford University Press. © 1963 by the
Board of Trustees of the Leland Stanford Junior University.

Cromwell's time, is a crime, though, in a minority of states, this is so only if it is open, notorious, or continuous. Fornication is not a criminal offence in England or in most countries of the civilized world, but only a minority of American states do not have statutes making fornication under certain conditions punishable, and some states make even a single act punishable.[1] Besides these statutory provisions there is an unknown quantity of local or municipal enactments which, in some cases, are more restrictive than the state laws, and though these are for that reason of doubtful validity, they have been enforced. In California the penal code does not make prostitution or fornication a crime, yet for many years persons have been convicted in Los Angeles under a local ordinance of the offence commonly known as "resorting," solely on proof that they used a room for fornication.[2]

No doubt much, and perhaps most, of this American legislation against sexual immorality is as dead a letter as it is commonly said to be. But the facts as to law enforcement are at present very hard to establish. In many states, California among them, the annual criminal statistics do not usually break down figures for sex crimes further than the two heads of "Rape" and "Other sexual offences." But in Boston as late as 1954 the sex laws were reported to receive "normal" enforcement, and in 1948 there were 248 arrests for adultery in that city.[3] No one, I think, should contemplate this situation with complacency, for in combination with inadequate published statistics the existence of criminal laws which are generally not enforced places formidable discriminatory powers in the hands of the police and prosecuting authorities.

Mill's critics have always pointed to the actual existence of laws punishing mere immorality as if this in some way threw doubt on his claim that the criminal law should not be used for this purpose. His defenders have indeed complained that the critics were here guilty of fallacious reasoning or irrelevance. John Morley, for example, in a vivid phrase said that in Stephen's book "a good deal of bustling ponderosity is devoted" to establishing the existence of laws of this sort; he thought that Stephen had simply failed to see that "the actual

---

[1] See, for a short summary, the American Law Institute, Model Penal Code, Tentative Draft No. 4, pp. 204–10.

[2] The State Supreme Court in December 1961 held the ordinance to be in conflict with the state laws and void. See in re *Carol Lane*, Crim. No. 6929, 57 A.C. 103, 18 *Cal. Rptr.* 33. This was confirmed after a rehearing on June 28, 1962. 22 *Cal. Rptr.* 857.

[3] American Law Institute, Model Penal Code, Tentative Draft No. 4, p. 205, n. 16.

existence of laws of any given kind is wholly irrelevant to Mr. Mill's contention, which is that it would be better if laws of such a kind did not exist."[4] In fact, neither Stephen (except in one place[5]) nor Lord Devlin, who also appeals to the actual content of English criminal law, is guilty of this form of the fallacy of arguing from what is to what should be, nor are they guilty of irrelevance. Stephen, when forced by Morley to state why he regarded his examples as relevant to the argument, explained that he thought it "not irrelevant to show that Mill was at issue with the practical conclusions to which most nations had been led by experience." In somewhat similar fashion Lord Devlin said:

Is the argument consistent or inconsistent with the fundamental principles of English law as it exists today? That is the first way of testing it though by no means a conclusive one. In the field of jurisprudence one is at liberty to overturn even fundamental conceptions if they are theoretically unsound. But to see how the argument fares under the existing law is a good starting point.[6]

Both writers, I think, in these perhaps not very perspicuous remarks, intend to invoke only the innocuous conservative principle that there is a presumption that common and long established institutions are likely to have merits not apparent to the rationalist philosopher. Nonetheless, when we examine some of the particular rules or principles of criminal law discussed at length by these writers, it is apparent that the use made of them is both confused and confusing. These examples are not drawn from the area of sexual morals, and certainly many, who would wish to align themselves with Mill and protest against the use of the criminal law to punish practices simply because they offend positive morality, might hesitate or refuse to jettison the particular rules of criminal law instanced by these writers. So if they are correctly classed as rules which can only be explained as designed to enforce morality their persuasive force is very considerable. We may indeed, to use Stephen's words, "be disposed to doubt" whether a principle that would condemn these particular rules could be right. But there are, I think, good reasons for disputing these writers' treatment of these rules as examples of the use of the law solely to enforce morality. We are not forced to choose between

---

[4] Quoted in *Liberty, Equality, Fraternity*, p. 166 n.
[5] *Ibid.*, pp. 171–72.
[6] *The Enforcement of Morals* (Oxford: Oxford University Press, 1959), p. 7.

jettisoning them or assenting to the principle that the criminal law may be used for that purpose. Some closer analysis than these authors give to these examples is, however, required, and to this I now turn.

PATERNALISM AND THE ENFORCEMENT
OF MORALITY

I shall start with an example stressed by Lord Devlin. He points out[7] that, subject to certain exceptions such as rape, the criminal law has never admitted the consent of the victim as a defence. It is not a defence to a charge of murder or a deliberate assault, and this is why euthanasia or mercy killing terminating a man's life at his own request is still murder. This is a rule of criminal law which many now would wish to retain, though they would also wish to object to the legal punishment of offences against positive morality which harm no one. Lord Devlin thinks that these attitudes are inconsistent, for he asserts of the rule under discussion, "There is only one explanation," and this is that "there are certain standards of behaviour or moral principles which society requires to be observed."[8] Among these are the sanctity of human life and presumably (since the rule applies to assaults) the physical integrity of the person. So in the case of this rule and a number of others Lord Devlin claims that the "function" of the criminal law is "to enforce a moral principle and nothing else."[9]

But this argument is not really cogent, for Lord Devlin's statement that "there is only one explanation" is simply not true. The rules excluding the victim's consent as a defence to charges of murder or assault may perfectly well be explained as a piece of paternalism, designed to protect individuals against themselves. Mill no doubt might have protested against a paternalistic policy of using the law to protect even a consenting victim from bodily harm nearly as much as he protested against laws used merely to enforce positive morality; but this does not mean that these two policies are identical. Indeed, Mill himself was very well aware of the difference between them: for in condemning interference with individual liberty except to prevent harm to others he mentions *separate* types of inadequate ground which have been proffered for the use of compulsion. He distinguishes "because it will be better for him" and "because it will make him

[7] *The Enforcement of Morals*, p. 8.
[8] *Ibid.*
[9] *Ibid.*, p. 9.

happier" from "because in the opinion of others it would be right."[10]

Lord Devlin says of the attitude of the criminal law to the victim's consent that if the law existed for the protection of the individual there would be no reason why he should avail himself of it if he did not want it.[11] But paternalism—the protection of people against themselves—is a perfectly coherent policy. Indeed, it seems very strange in mid-twentieth century to insist upon this, for the wane of laissez faire since Mill's day is one of the commonplaces of social history, and instances of paternalism now abound in our law, criminal and civil. The supply of drugs or narcotics, even to adults, except under medical prescription is punishable by the criminal law, and it would seem very dogmatic to say of the law creating this offence that "there is only one explanation," namely, that the law was concerned not with the protection of the would-be purchasers against themselves, but only with the punishment of the seller for his immorality. If, as seems obvious, paternalism is a possible explanation of such laws, it is also possible in the case of the rule excluding the consent of the victim as a defence to a charge of assault. In neither case are we forced to conclude with Lord Devlin that the law's "function" is "to enforce a moral principle and nothing else."[12]

In Chapter 5 of his essay Mill carried his protests against paternalism to lengths that may now appear to us fantastic. He cites the example of restrictions of the sale of drugs, and criticises them as interferences with the liberty of the would-be purchaser rather than with that of the seller. No doubt if we no longer sympathise with this criticism this is due, in part, to a general decline in the belief that individuals know their own interests best, and to an increased awareness of a great range of factors which diminish the significance to be attached to an apparently free choice or to consent. Choices may be made or consent given without adequate reflection or appreciation of the consequences; or in pursuit of merely transitory desires; or in various predicaments when the judgment is likely to be clouded; or under inner psychological compulsion; or under pressure by others of a kind too subtle to be susceptible of proof in a law court. Underlying Mill's extreme fear of paternalism there perhaps is a conception of what a normal human being is like which now seems not to correspond to the facts. Mill, in fact, endows him with too much of the psychol-

---

[10] *On Liberty*, Chapter I.
[11] *The Enforcement of Morals*, p. 8.
[12] See, for other possible explanations of these rules, Hughes, "Morals and the Criminal Law," *Yale Law Journal*, Vol. 71, p. 670.

ogy of a middle-aged man whose desires are relatively fixed, not liable to be artificially stimulated by external influences; who knows what he wants and what gives him satisfaction or happiness; and who pursues these things when he can.

Certainly a modification in Mill's principles is required, if they are to accommodate the rule of criminal law under discussion or other instances of paternalism. But the modified principles would not abandon the objection to the use of the criminal law merely to enforce positive morality. They would only have to provide that harming others is something we may still seek to prevent by use of the criminal law, even when the victims consent to or assist in the acts which are harmful to them. The neglect of the distinction between paternalism and what I have termed legal moralism is important as a form of a more general error. It is too often assumed that if a law is not designed to protect one man from another its only rationale can be that it is designed to punish moral wickedness or, in Lord Devlin's words, "to enforce a moral principle." Thus it is often urged that statutes punishing cruelty to animals can only be explained in that way. But it is certainly intelligible, both as an account of the original motives inspiring such legislation and as the specification of an aim widely held to be worth pursuing, to say that the law is here concerned with the *suffering*, albeit only of animals, rather than with the immorality of torturing them.[13] Certainly no one who supports this use of the criminal law is thereby bound in consistency to admit that the law may punish forms of immorality which involve no suffering to any sentient being.

[13] Lord Devlin seems quite unaccountably to ignore this point in his brief reference to cruelty to animals, *The Enforcement of Morals*, p. 17.

SELECTIONS FROM *PRINCIPLES OF POLITICAL ECONOMY**

J. S. Mill

✦

[*Free enterprise, socialism, and liberty.*]

. . . We are too ignorant either of what individual agency in its best form, or Socialism in its best form, can accomplish, to be qualified to decide which of the two will be the ultimate form of human society.

If a conjecture may be hazarded, the decision will probably depend mainly on one consideration, viz. which of the two systems is consistent with the greatest amount of human liberty and spontaneity. After the means of subsistence are assured, the next in strength of the personal wants of human beings is liberty; and (unlike the physical wants, which as civilization advances become more moderate and more amenable to control) it increases instead of diminishing in intensity as the intelligence and the moral faculties are more developed. The perfection both of social arrangements and of practical morality would be, to secure to all persons complete independence and freedom of action, subject to no restriction but that of not doing injury to others: and the education which taught or the social institutions which required them to exchange the control of their own actions for any amount of comfort or affluence, or to renounce liberty for the sake of equality, would deprive them of one of the most elevated characteristics of human nature. It remains to be discovered how far the preservation of this characteristic would be found compatible with the

---

* From the seventh edition, originally published 1871. The first edition was published in 1848. Mill introduced extensive revisions in subsequent editions. The seventh edition can be found in most libraries in a convenient single volume edited by W. S. Ashley in 1909 and reprinted many times. The Ashley volume indicates major changes from edition to edition. The definitive edition, based on the seventh edition but noting all variants, forms Vols. II and III of the *Collected Works of John Stuart Mill* (University of Toronto Press, 1965) and was prepared by J. M. Robson. The subheadings of the selections have been added by the present editor.

64

Communistic organization of society. No doubt this, like all the other objections to the Socialist schemes, is vastly exaggerated. The members of the association need not be required to live together more than they do now, nor need they be controlled in the disposal of their individual share of the produce, and of the probably large amount of leisure which, if they limited their production to things really worth producing, they would possess. Individuals need not be chained to an occupation, or to a particular locality. The restraints of Communism would be freedom in comparison with the present condition of the majority of the human race. The generality of labourers in this and most other countries have as little choice of occupation or freedom of locomotion, are practically as dependent on fixed rules and on the will of others, as they could be on any system short of actual slavery; to say nothing of the entire domestic subjection of one half the species, to which it is the signal honour of Owenism and most other forms of Socialism that they assign equal rights, in all respects, with those of the hitherto dominant sex. But it is not by comparison with the present bad state of society that the claims of Communism can be estimated; nor is it sufficient that it should promise greater personal and mental freedom than is now enjoyed by those who have not enough of either to deserve the name. The question is, whether there would be any asylum left for individuality of character; whether public opinion would not be a tyrannical yoke; whether the absolute dependence of each on all, and surveillance of each by all, would not grind all down into a tame uniformity of thoughts, feelings, and actions. This is already one of the glaring evils of the existing state of society, notwithstanding a much greater diversity of education and pursuits, and a much less absolute dependence of the individual on the mass, than would exist in the Communistic regime. No society in which eccentricity is a matter of reproach can be in a wholesome state. It is yet to be ascertained whether the Communistic scheme would be consistent with that multiform development of human nature, those manifold unlikenesses, that diversity of tastes and talents, and variety of intellectual points of view, which not only form a great part of the interest of human life, but by bringing intellects into stimulating collision, and by presenting to each innumerable notions that he would not have conceived of himself, are the mainspring of mental and moral progression. [Book II, Chapter I, §3.][1]

---

[1] Substantial changes were made in this section in the 3rd edition and preserved in subsequent editions.

[*Some functions of government.*]

. . . There is a multitude of cases in which governments, with general approbation, assume powers and execute functions for which no reason can be assigned, except the simple one, that they conduct to general convenience. We may take as an example, the function (which is a monopoly too) of coining money. This is assumed for no more recondite purpose than that of saving to individuals the trouble, delay, and expense of weighing and assaying. No one, however, even of those most jealous of state interference, has objected to this as an improper exercise of the powers of government. Prescribing a set of standard weights and measures is another instance. Paving, lighting, and cleansing the streets and thoroughfares is another; whether done by the general government, or, as is more usual, and generally more advisable, by a municipal authority. Making or improving harbours, building lighthouses, making surveys in order to have accurate maps and charts, raising dykes to keep the sea out, and embankments to keep rivers in, are cases in point.

Examples might be indefinitely multiplied without intruding on any disputed ground. But enough has been said to show that the admitted functions of government embrace a much wider field than can easily be included within the ring-fence of any restrictive definition, and that it is hardly possible to find any ground of justification common to them all, except the comprehensive one of general expediency; nor to limit the interference of government by any universal rule, save the simple and vague one, that it should never be but when the case of expediency is strong. [Book V, Chapter I, §2.]

[*Types of government intervention.*]

We have now reached the last part of our undertaking; the discussion, so far as suited to this treatise (that is, so far as it is a question of principle, not detail), of the limits of the province of government: the question, to what objects governmental intervention in the affairs of society may or should extend, over and above those which necessarily appertain to it. No subject has been more keenly contested in the present age: the contest, however, has chiefly taken place round certain select points, with only flying excursions into the rest of the field. Those indeed who have discussed any particular question of government interference, such as state education (spiritual or secular), regulation of hours of labour, a public provision for the poor, &c., have often dealt largely in general arguments, far outstretching the special application made of them, and have shown a sufficiently strong bias either in favour of letting things alone, or in favour of meddling; but have seldom declared, or apparently decided in their own minds, how far they would carry either principle. The supporters of interference have been content with asserting a general right and duty on the part of government to intervene, wherever its intervention would be useful: and when those who have been called the *laisser-faire* school have attempted any definite limitation of the province of government, they have usually restricted it to the protection of person and property against force and fraud; a definition to which neither they nor any one else can deliberately adhere, since it excludes, as has been shown in a preceding chapter (Supra, book V. ch. 1), some of the most indispensable and unanimously recognized of the duties of government.

Without professing entirely to supply this deficiency of a general theory, on a question which does not, as I conceive, admit of any universal solution, I shall attempt to afford some little aid towards the resolution of this class of questions as they arise, by examining, in the most general point of view in which the subject can be considered, what are the advantages, and what the evils or inconveniences, of government interference.

We must set out by distinguishing between two kinds of intervention by the government, which, though they may relate to the same subject, differ widely in their nature and effects, and require, for their justification, motives of a very different degree of urgency. The intervention may extend to controlling the free agency of individuals. Government may interdict all persons from doing certain things; or from doing them without its authorization; or may prescribe to them certain things to be done, or a certain manner of doing things which it is left optional with them to do or to abstain from. This is the *authoritative* interference of government. There is another kind of intervention which is not authoritative: when a government, instead of issuing a command and enforcing it by penalties, adopts the course so seldom resorted to by governments, and of which such important use might be made, that of giving advice, and promulgating information; or when, leaving individuals free to use their own means of pursuing any object of general interest, the government, not meddling with them, but not trusting the object solely to their care, establishes, side by side with their arrangements, an agency of its own for a like purpose. Thus, it is one thing to maintain a Church Establishment, and another to refuse toleration to other religions, or to persons professing no religion. It is one thing to provide schools or colleges, and another to require that no person shall act as an instructor of youth without a government licence. There might be a national bank, or a government manufactory, without any monopoly against private banks and manufactories. There might be a post-office, without penalties against the conveyance of letters by other means. There may be a corps of government engineers for civil purposes, while the profession of a civil engineer is free to be adopted by every one. There may be public hospitals, without any restriction upon private medical or surgical practice.

It is evident, even at first sight, that the authoritative form of government intervention has a much more limited sphere of legitimate action than the other. It requires a much stronger necessity to justify it in any case; while there are large departments of human life from which it must be unreservedly and imperiously excluded. Whatever theory we adopt respecting the foundation of the social union, and under whatever political institutions we live there is a circle around every individual human being which no government, be it that of one, of a few, or of the many, ought to be permitted to overstep: there is a part of the life of every person who has come to years of discretion, within which the individuality of that person ought to reign uncontrolled either by any other individual or by the public collectively. That there is, or ought to be, some space in human existence thus entrenched around, and sacred from authoritative intrusion, no one who professes the smallest regard to human freedom or dignity will call in question: the point to be determined is, where the limit should be placed; how large a province of human life this reserved territory should include. I apprehend that it ought to include all that part which concerns only the life, whether inward or outward, of the individual, and does not affect the interests of others, or affects them only through the moral influence of example. With respect to the domain of the inward consciousness, the thoughts and feelings, and as much of external conduct as is personal only, involving no consequences, none at least of a painful or injurious kind, to other people; I hold that it is allowable in all, and in the more thoughtful and cultivated often a duty, to assert and promulgate, with all the force they are capable of, their opinion of what is good or bad, admirable or contemptible, but not to compel others to that opinion; whether the force used is that of extra-legal coercion, or exerts itself by means of the law.

Even in those portions of conduct which do affect the interest of others, the onus of making out a case always lies on the defenders of legal prohibitions. It is not a merely constructive or presumptive injury to others which will justify the interference of law with individual freedom. To be prevented from doing what one is inclined to, or from acting according to one's own judgment of what is desirable, is not only always irksome, but always tends, *pro tanto*, to starve the development of some portion of the bodily or mental faculties, either sensitive or active; and unless the conscience of the individual goes freely with the legal restraint, it partakes, either in a great or in a small degree, of the degradation of slavery. Scarcely any degree of utility, short of absolute necessity, will justify a prohibitory regulation, unless it can also be made to recommend itself to the general conscience; unless persons of ordinary good intentions either believe already, or can be induced to believe, that the thing prohibited is a thing which they ought not to wish to do.

It is otherwise with governmental interferences which do not restrain individual free agency. When a government provides means for fulfilling a certain end, leaving individuals free to avail themselves of different means if in their opinion preferable, there is no infringement of liberty, no irksome or degrading restraint. One of the principal objections to government interference is then absent. There is, however, in almost all forms of government agency, one thing which is compulsory; the provision of the pecuniary means. These are derived from taxation; or, if existing in the form of an endowment derived from public property, they are still the cause of as much compulsory taxation as the sale or the annual proceeds of the property would enable to be dispensed with.[2] And the objection necessarily attaching to compulsory contributions, is almost always greatly aggravated by the expensive precautions and onerous restrictions which are indispensable to prevent evasion of a compulsory tax. [Book V, Chapter XI, §1–2.]

[*Some exceptions to the* laisser-faire *principle.*]

Now, the proposition that the consumer is a competent judge of the commodity, can be admitted only with numerous abatements and exceptions. He is generally the best judge (though even this is not true universally) of the material objects produced for his use. These are

---

[2] The only cases in which government agency involves nothing of a compulsory nature, are the rare cases in which, without any artificial monopoly, it pays its own expenses. A bridge built with public money, on which tolls are collected sufficient to pay not only all current expenses, but the interest of the original outlay, is one case in point. The government railways in Belgium and Germany are another example. The Post Office, if its monopoly were abolished, and it still paid its expenses, would be another.

destined to supply some physical want, or gratify some taste or inclination, respecting which wants or inclinations there is no appeal from the
person who feels them; or they are the means and appliances of some
occupation, for the use of the persons engaged in it, who may be
presumed to be judges of the things required in their own habitual
employment. But there are other things, of the worth of which the
demand of the market is by no means a test; things of which the utility
does not consist in ministering to inclinations, nor in serving the daily
uses of life, and the want of which is least felt where the need is
greatest. This is peculiarly true of those things which are chiefly useful
as tending to raise the character of human beings. The uncultivated
cannot be competent judges of cultivation. Those who most need to be
made wiser and better, usually desire it least, and, if they desired it,
would be incapable of finding the way to it by their own lights. It will
continually happen, on the voluntary system, that, the end not being
desired, the means will not be provided at all, or that, the persons
requiring improvement having an imperfect or altogether erroneous
conception of what they want, the supply called forth by the demand
of the market will be anything but what is really required. Now any
well-intentioned and tolerably civilized government may think, without presumption, that it does or ought to possess a degree of cultivation above the average of the community which it rules, and that it
should therefore be capable of offering better education and better
instruction to the people, than the greater number of them would
spontaneously demand. Education, therefore, is one of those things
which it is admissible in principle that a government should provide
for the people. The case is one to which the reasons of the non-interference principle do not necessarily or universally extend.[3]

---

[3] In opposition to these opinions, a writer, with whom on many points I
agree, but whose hostility to government intervention seems to me too indiscrimi-
nate and unqualified, M. Dunoyer, observes, that instruction, however good in
itself, can only be useful to the public in so far as they are willing to receive it,
and that the best proof that the instruction is suitable to their wants is its success
as a pecuniary enterprise. This argument seems no more conclusive respecting
instruction for the mind, than it would be respecting medicine for the body. No
medicine will do the patient any good if he cannot be induced to take it; but we
are not bound to admit as a corollary from this, that the patient will select the
right medicine without assistance. Is it not probable that a recommendation, from
any quarter which he respects, may induce him to accept a better medicine than
he would spontaneously have chosen? This is, in respect to education, the very
point in debate. Without doubt, instruction which is so far in advance of the
people that they cannot be induced to avail themselves of it, is to them of no more
worth than if it did not exist. But between what they spontaneously choose, and
what they will refuse to accept when offered, there is a breadth of interval

. . . A second exception to the doctrine that individuals are the best judges of their own interest, is when an individual attempts to decide irrevocably now what will be best for his interest at some future and distant time. The presumption in favour of individual judgment is only legitimate, where the judgment is grounded on actual, and especially on present, personal experience; not where it is formed antecedently to experience, and not suffered to be reversed even after experience has condemned it. When persons have bound themselves by a contract, not simply to do some one thing, but to continue doing something for ever or for a prolonged period, without any power of revoking the engagement, the presumption which their perseverance in that course of conduct would otherwise raise in favour of its being advantageous to them, does not exist; and any such presumption which can be grounded on their having voluntarily entered into the contract, perhaps at an early age, and without any real knowledge of what they undertook, is commonly next to null. The practical maxim of leaving contracts free is not applicable without great limitations in case of engagements in perpetuity; and the law should be extremely jealous of such engagements; and should refuse its sanction to them, when the obligations they impose are such as the contracting party cannot be a competent judge of; if it ever does sanction them, it should take every possible security for their being contracted with foresight and deliberation; and in compensation for not permitting the parties themselves to revoke their engagement, should grant them a release from it, on a sufficient case being made out before an impartial authority. These considerations are eminently applicable to marriage, the most important of all cases of engagement for life. . . .

To a fourth case of exception I must request particular attention, it being one to which, as it appears to me, the attention of political economists has not yet been sufficiently drawn. There are matters in

---

proportioned to their deference for the recommender. Besides, a thing of which the public are bad judges may require to be shown to them and pressed on their attention for a long time, and to prove its advantages by long experience, before they learn to appreciate it, yet they may learn at last; which they might never have done, if the thing had not been thus obtruded upon them in act, but only recommended in theory. Now, a pecuniary speculation cannot wait years, or perhaps generations for success; it must succeed rapidly, or not at all. Another consideration which M. Dunoyer seems to have overlooked, is, that institutions and modes of tuition which never could be made sufficiently popular to repay, with a profit, the expenses incurred on them, may be invaluable to the many by giving the highest quality of education to the few, and keeping up the perpetual succession of superior minds, by whom knowledge is advanced, and the community urged forward in civilization.

which the interference of law is required, not to overrule the judgment of individuals respecting their own interest, but to give effect to that judgment: they being unable to give effect to it except by concert, which concert again cannot be effectual unless it receives validity and sanction from the law. For illustration, and without prejudging the particular point, I may advert to the question of diminishing the hours of labour. Let us suppose, what is at least supposable, whether it be the fact or not—that a general reduction of the hours of factory labour, say from ten to nine, would be for the advantage of the workpeople: that they would receive as high wages, or nearly as high, for nine hours' labour as they receive for ten. If this would be the result, and if the operatives generally are convinced that it would, the limitation, some may say, will be adopted spontaneously. I answer, that it will not be adopted unless the body of operatives bind themselves to one another to abide by it. A workman who refused to work more than nine hours while there were others who worked ten, would either not be employed at all, or if employed, must submit to lose one-tenth of his wages. However convinced, therefore, he may be that it is the interest of the class to work short time, it is contrary to his own interest to set the example, unless he is well assured that all or most others will follow it. But suppose a general agreement of the whole class: might not this be effectual without the sanction of law? Not unless enforced by opinion with a rigour practically equal to that of law. For however beneficial the observance of the regulation might be to the class collectively, the immediate interest of every individual would lie in violating it: and the more numerous those who adhered to the rule, the more would individuals gain by departing from it. If nearly all restricted themselves to nine hours, those who chose to work for ten would gain all the advantages of the restriction, together with the profit of infringing it; they would get ten hours' wages for nine hours' work, and an hour's wages besides. I grant that if a large majority adhered to the nine hours, there would be no harm done: the benefit would be, in the main secured to the class, while those individuals who preferred to work harder and earn more, would have an opportunity of doing so. This certainly would be the state of things to be wished for; and assuming that a reduction of hours without any diminution of wages could take place without expelling the commodity from some of its markets—which is in every particular instance a question of fact, not of principle—the manner in which it would be most desirable that this effect should be brought about, would be by a quiet change in the general custom of the trade; short hours becoming, by spontaneous choice, the general practice, but those who chose to deviate from it having the fullest liberty to do so. Probably, however, so many would prefer the ten hours' work on the improved terms, that the limitation could not be maintained as a general practice: what some did from choice, others would soon be obliged to do from necessity, and those who had chosen long hours for the sake of increased wages, would be forced in the end to work long hours for no greater wages than before. Assuming then that it really would be the interest of each to work only nine hours if he could be assured that all others would do the same, there might be no means of their attaining this object but by converting their supposed mutual agreement into an engagement under penalty, by consenting to have it enforced by law. I am not expressing any opinion in favour of such an enactment, which has never in this country been demanded, and which I certainly should not, in present circumstances, recommend: but it serves to exemplify the manner in which classes of persons may need the assistance of law, to give effect to their deliberate collective opinion of their own interest, by affording to every individual a guarantee that his competitors will pursue the same course, without which he cannot safely adopt it himself. . . . [Book V, Chapter XI, §§8–12.]

THE NOTION OF
"NEGATIVE" FREEDOM*

Isaiah Berlin

✢

I am normally said to be free to the degree to which no human being interferes with my activity. Political liberty in this sense is simply the area within which a man can do what he wants. If I am prevented by other persons from doing what I want I am to that degree unfree; and if the area within which I can do what I want is contracted by other men beyond a certain minimum, I can be described as being coerced, or, it may be, enslaved. Coercion is not, however, a term that covers every form of inability. If I say that I am unable to jump more than 10 feet in the air, or cannot read because I am blind, or cannot understand the darker pages of Hegel, it would be eccentric to say that I am to that degree enslaved or coerced. Coercion implies the deliberate interference of other human beings within the area in which I wish to act. You lack political liberty or freedom only if you are prevented from attaining your goal by human beings.[1] Mere incapacity to attain your goal is not lack of political freedom.[2] This is brought out by the use of such modern expressions as 'economic freedom' and its counterpart, 'economic slavery.' It is argued, very plausibly, that if a man is too poor to afford something on which there is no legal ban—a loaf of bread, a journey round the world, recourse to the law courts—he is as little free to have it as he would be if it were forbidden him by law. If my poverty were a kind of disease, which prevented me from buying bread or paying for the journey round the world, or getting my case heard, as lameness prevents me from running, this inability would not naturally be described as a lack of freedom at all, least of all political

---

* From *Two Concepts of Liberty* by Isaiah Berlin (London: Oxford University Press, 1958), pp. 7–16. Reprinted by permission of The Clarendon Press, Oxford.

[1] I do not, of course, mean to imply the truth of the converse.

[2] Helvétius made this point very clearly: 'The free man is the man who is not in irons, nor imprisoned in a gaol, nor terrorized like a slave by the fear of punishment . . . it is not lack of freedom not to fly like an eagle or swim like a whale.'

freedom. It is only because I believe that my inability to get what I want is due to the fact that other human beings have made arrangements whereby I am, whereas others are not, prevented from having enough money with which to pay for it, that I think myself a victim of coercion or slavery. In other words, this use of the term depends on a particular social and economic theory about the causes of my poverty or weakness. If my lack of means is due to my lack of mental or physical capacity, then I begin to speak of being deprived of freedom (and not simply of poverty) only if I accept the theory.[3] If, in addition, I believe that I am being kept in want by a definite arrangement which I consider unjust or unfair, I speak of economic slavery or oppression. 'The nature of things does not madden us, only ill will does', said Rousseau. The criterion of oppression is the part that I believe to be played by other human beings, directly or indirectly, in frustrating my wishes. By being free in this sense I mean not being interfered with by others. The wider the area of non-interference the wider my freedom.

This is certainly what the classical English political philosophers meant when they used this word.[4] They disagreed about how wide the area could or should be. They supposed that it could not, as things were, be unlimited, because if it were, it would entail a state in which all men could boundlessly interfere with all other men; and this kind of 'natural' freedom would lead to social chaos in which men's minimum needs would not be satisfied; or else the liberties of the weak would be suppressed by the strong. Because they perceived that human purposes and activities do not automatically harmonize with one another; and, because (whatever their official doctrines) they put high value on other goals, such as justice, or happiness, or security, or varying degrees of equality, they were prepared to curtail freedom in the interests of other values and, indeed, of freedom itself. For, without this, it was impossible to create the kind of association that they thought desirable. Consequently, it is assumed by these thinkers that the area of men's free action must be limited by law. But equally it is assumed, especially by such libertarians as Locke and Mill in England, and Constant and Tocqueville in France, that there ought to exist a

---

[3] The Marxist conception of social laws is, of course, the best-known version of this theory, but it forms a large element in some Christian and utilitarian, and all socialist, doctrines.

[4] 'A free man,' said Hobbes, 'is he that . . . is not hindered to do what he hath the will to do.' Law is always a 'fetter', even if it protects you from being bound in chains that are heavier than those of the law, say, arbitrary despotism or chaos. Bentham says much the same.

certain minimum area of personal freedom which must on no account be violated, for if it is overstepped, the individual will find himself in an area too narrow for even that minimum development of his natural faculties which alone makes it possible to pursue, and even to conceive, the various ends which men hold good or right or sacred. It follows that a frontier must be drawn between the area of private life and that of public authority. Where it is to be drawn is a matter of argument, indeed of haggling. Men are largely interdependent, and no man's activity is so completely private as never to obstruct the lives of others in any way. 'Freedom for the pike is death for the minnows'; the liberty of some must depend on the restraint of others.[5] Still, a practical compromise has to be found.

[5] 'Freedom for an Oxford don', others have been known to add, 'is a very different thing from freedom for an Egyptian peasant.'

This proposition derives its force from something that is both true and important, but the phrase itself remains a piece of political claptrap. It is true that to offer political rights, or safeguards against intervention by the state, to men who are half-naked, illiterate, underfed, and diseased is to mock their condition; they need medical help or education before they can understand, or make use of, an increase in their freedom. First things come first: there are situations, as a nineteenth-century Russian radical writer declared, in which boots are superior to the works of Shakespeare; individual freedom is not everyone's primary need. For freedom is not the mere absence of frustration of whatever kind; this would inflate the meaning of the word until it meant too much or too little. The Egyptian peasant needs clothes or medicine before, and more than, personal liberty, but the minimum freedom that he needs today, and the greater degree of freedom that he may need tomorrow, is not some species of freedom peculiar to him, but identical with that of professors, artists, and millionaires.

What troubles the consciences of Western liberals is not, I think, the belief that the freedom that men seek differs according to their social or economic conditions, but that the minority who possess it have gained it by exploiting or, at least, averting their gaze from the vast majority who do not. They believe, with good reason, that if individual liberty is an ultimate end for human beings, none should be deprived of it by others; least of all that some should enjoy it at the expense of others. Equality of liberty; not to treat others as I should not wish them to treat me; repayment of my debt to those who alone have made possible my liberty or prosperity or enlightenment; justice, in its simplest and most universal sense—these are the foundations of liberal morality. Liberty is not the only goal of men. I can, like the Russian critic Belinsky, say that if others are to be deprived of it—if my brothers are to remain in poverty, squalor, and chains— then I do not want it for myself, I reject it with both hands, and infinitely prefer to share their fate. But nothing is gained by a confusion of terms. To avoid glaring inequality or widespread misery I am ready to sacrifice some, or all, of my freedom: I may do so willingly and freely: but it is freedom that I am giving up for the sake of justice or equality or the love of my fellow men. I should be guilt-stricken, and rightly so, if I were not, in some circumstances, ready to make this sacrifice. But a sacrifice is not an increase in what is being sacrificed, namely freedom, however great the moral need or the compensation for it. Everything is what it is: liberty is liberty, not equality or fairness or justice or human happiness or a quiet conscience. If the liberty of myself or my class or nation depends on the misery of a vast number of other human beings, the system which promotes

Philosophers with an optimistic view of human nature, and a belief in the possibility of harmonizing human interests, such as Locke or Adam Smith and, in some moods, Mill, believed that social harmony and progress were compatible with reserving a large area for private life over which neither the state nor any other authority must be allowed to trespass. Hobbes, and those who agreed with him, especially conservative or reactionary thinkers, argued that if men were to be prevented from destroying one another, and making social life a jungle or a wilderness, greater safeguards must be instituted to keep them in their places, and wished correspondingly to increase the area of centralized control, and decrease that of the individual. But both sides agreed that some portion of human existence must remain independent of the sphere of social control. To invade that preserve, however small, would be despotism. The most eloquent of all defenders of freedom and privacy, Benjamin Constant, who had not forgotten the Jacobin dictatorship, declared that at the very least the liberty of religion, opinion, expression, property, must be guaranteed against arbitrary invasion. Jefferson, Burke, Paine, Mill, compiled different catalogues of individual liberties, but the argument for keeping authority at bay is always substantially the same. We must preserve a minimum area of personal freedom if we are not to 'degrade or deny our nature'. We cannot remain absolutely free, and must give up some of our liberty to preserve the rest. But total self-surrender is self-defeating. What then must the minimum be? That which a man cannot give up without offending against the essence of his human nature. What is this essence? What are the standards which it entails? This has been, and perhaps always will be, a matter of infinite debate. But whatever the principle in terms of which the area of non-interference is to be drawn, whether it is that of natural law or natural rights, or of utility or the pronouncements of a categorical imperative, or the sanctity of the social contract, or any other concept with which men have sought to clarify and justify their convictions, liberty in this sense means liberty *from*; absence of interference beyond the shifting, but always recognizable, frontier. 'The only freedom which deserves the name is

---

this is unjust and immoral. But if I curtail or lose my freedom, in order to lessen the shame of such inequality, and do not thereby materially increase the individual liberty of others, an absolute loss of liberty occurs. This may be compensated for by a gain in justice or in happiness or in peace, but the loss remains, and it is nothing but a confusion of values to say that although my 'liberal,' individual freedom may go by the board, some other kind of freedom—'social' or 'economic' —is increased. But it remains true that the freedom of some must at times be curtailed to secure the freedom of others. Upon what principle should this be done? If freedom is a sacred, untouchable value, there can be no such absolute principle.

that of pursuing our own good in our own way', said the most celebrated of its champions. If this is so, is compulsion ever justified? Mill had no doubt that it was. Since justice demands that all individuals be entitled to a minimum of freedom, all other individuals were of necessity to be restrained, if need be by force, from depriving anyone of it. Indeed, the whole function of law was the prevention of just such collisions: the state was reduced to what Lassalle contemptuously described as the functions of a nightwatchman or traffic policeman.

What made the protection of individual liberty so sacred to Mill? In his famous essay he declares that unless men are left to live as they wish 'in the path which merely concerns themselves', civilization cannot advance; the truth will not, for lack of a free market in ideas, come to light; there will be no scope for spontaneity, originality, genius, for mental energy, for moral courage. Society will be crushed by the weight of 'collective mediocrity'. Whatever is rich and diversified will be crushed by the weight of custom, by men's constant tendency to conformity, which breeds only 'withered capacities', 'pinched and hidebound', 'cramped and warped' human beings. 'Pagan self-assertion is as worthy as Christian self-denial.' 'All the errors which a man is likely to commit against advice and warning are far outweighed by the evil of allowing others to constrain him to what they deem is good.' The defence of liberty consists in the 'negative' goal of warding off interference. To threaten a man with persecution unless he submits to a life in which he exercises no choices of his goals; to block before him every door but one, no matter how noble the prospect upon which it opens, or how benevolent the motives of those who arrange this, is to sin against the truth that he is a man, a being with a life of his own to live. This is liberty as it has been conceived by liberals in the modern world from the days of Erasmus (some would say of Occam) to our own. Every plea for civil liberties and individual rights, every protest against exploitation and humiliation, against the encroachment of public authority, or the mass hypnosis of custom or organized propaganda, springs from this individualistic, and much disputed, conception of man.

Three facts about this position may be noted. In the first place Mill confuses two distinct notions. One is that all coercion is, in so far as it frustrates human desires, bad as such, although it may have to be applied to prevent other, greater evils; while non-interference, which is the opposite of coercion, is good as such, although it is not the only good. This is the 'negative' conception of liberty in its classical form. The other is that men should seek to discover the truth, or to develop a certain type of character of which Mill approved—fearless, original, imaginative, independent, non-conforming to the point of eccentricity, and so on—and that truth can be found, and such character can be bred, only in conditions of freedom. Both these are liberal views, but they are not identical, and the connexion between them is, at best, empirical. No one would argue that truth or freedom of self-expression could flourish where dogma crushes all thought. But the evidence of history tends to show (as, indeed, was argued by James Stephen in his formidable attack on Mill in his *Liberty, Equality, Fraternity*) that integrity, love of truth and fiery individualism grow at least as often in severely disciplined communities among, for example, the puritan Calvinists of Scotland or New England, or under military discipline, as in more tolerant or indifferent societies; and if this is so accepted, Mill's argument for liberty as a necessary condition for the growth of human genius falls to the ground. If his two goals proved incompatible, Mill would be faced with a cruel dilemma, quite apart from the further difficulties created by the inconsistency of his doctrines with strict utilitarianism, even in his own humane version of it.[6]

In the second place, the doctrine is comparatively modern. There seems to be scarcely any consciousness of individual liberty as a political ideal in the ancient world. Condorcet has already remarked that the notion of individual rights is absent from the legal conceptions of the Romans and Greeks; this seems to hold equally of the Jewish, Chinese, and all other ancient civilizations that have since come to light.[7] The domination of this ideal has been the exception rather than the rule, even in the recent history of the West. Nor has liberty in this sense often formed a rallying cry for the great masses of mankind. The desire not to be impinged upon, to be left to oneself, has been a mark of high civilization both on the part of individuals and communities. The sense of privacy itself, of the area of personal relationships as something sacred in its own right, derives from a conception of freedom which, for all its religious roots, is scarcely older, in its developed state, than the Renaissance or the Reformation.[8] Yet its

---

[6] This is but another illustration of the natural tendency of all but a very few thinkers to believe that all the things they hold good must be intimately connected, or at least compatible, with one another. The history of thought, like the history of nations, is strewn with examples of inconsistent, or at least disparate, elements artificially yoked together in a despotic system, or held together by the danger of some common enemy. In due course the danger passes, and conflicts between the allies arise, which often disrupt the system, sometimes to the great benefit of mankind.

[7] See the valuable discussion of this in Michel Villey, *Leçons d'Histoire de la Philosophie du Droit,* who traces the embryo of the notion of subjective rights to Occam.

[8] Christian (and Jewish or Moslem) belief in the absolute authority of divine or natural laws, or in the equality of all men in the sight of God, is very different from belief in freedom to live as one prefers.

decline would mark the death of a civilization, of an entire moral outlook.

The third characteristic of this notion of liberty is of greater importance. It is that liberty in this sense is not incompatible with some kinds of autocracy, or at any rate with the absence of self-government. Liberty in this sense is principally concerned with the area of control, not with its source. Just as a democracy may, in fact, deprive the individual citizen of a great many liberties which he might have in some other form of society, so it is perfectly conceivable that a liberal-minded despot would allow his subjects a large measure of personal freedom. The despot who leaves his subjects a wide area of liberty may be unjust, or encourage the wildest inequalities, care little for order, or virtue, or knowledge; but provided he does not curb their liberty, or at least curbs it less than many other regimes, he meets with Mill's specification.[9] Freedom in this sense is not, at any rate logically, connected with democracy or self-government. Self-government may, on the whole, provide a better guarantee of the preservation of civil liberties than other regimes, and has been defended as such by libertarians. But there is no necessary connexion between individual liberty and democratic rule. The answer to the question 'Who governs me?' is logically distinct from the question 'How far does government interfere with me?' It is in this difference that the great contrast between the two concepts of negative and positive liberty, in the end, consists.[10] For the 'positive' sense of liberty comes to light if we try to

---

[9] Indeed, it is arguable that in the Prussia of Frederick the Great or in the Austria of Josef II, men of imagination, originality, and creative genius, and, indeed, minorities of all kinds, were less persecuted and felt the pressure, both of institutions and custom, less heavy upon them than in many an earlier or later democracy.

[10] 'Negative liberty' is something the extent of which, in a given case, it is difficult to estimate. It might, *prima facie*, seem to depend simply on the power to choose between at any rate two alternatives. Nevertheless, not all choices are equally free, or free at all. If in a totalitarian state I betray my friend under threat of torture, perhaps even if I act from fear of losing my job, I can reasonably say that I did not act freely. Nevertheless, I did, of course, make a choice, and could, at any rate in theory, have chosen to be killed or tortured or imprisoned. The mere existence of alternatives is not, therefore, enough to make my action free (although it may be voluntary) in the normal sense of the word. The extent of my freedom seems to depend on (*a*) how many possibilities are open to me (although the method of counting these can never be more than impressionistic. Possibilities of action are not discrete entities like apples, which can be exhaustively enumerated); (*b*) how easy or difficult each of these possibilities is to actualize; (*c*) how important in my plan of life, given my character and circumstances, these possibilities are when compared with each other; (*d*) how far they are closed and opened by deliberate human acts; (*e*) what value not merely the agent, but the general sentiment of the society in which he lives, puts on the

answer the question, not 'What am I free to do or be?', but 'By whom am I ruled?' or 'Who is to say what I am, and what I am not, to be or do?' The connexion between democracy and individual liberty is a good deal more tenuous than it seemed to many advocates of both. The desire to be governed by myself, or at any rate to participate in the process by which my life is to be controlled, may be as deep a wish as that of a free area for action, and perhaps historically older. But it is not a desire for the same thing. So different is it, indeed, as to have led in the end to the great clash of ideologies that dominates our world. For it is this—the 'positive' conception of liberty: not freedom from, but freedom to—which the adherents of the 'negative' notion represent as being, at times, no better than a specious disguise for brutal tyranny.

---

various possibilities. All these magnitudes must be 'integrated,' and a conclusion, necessarily never precise, or indisputable, drawn from this process. It may well be that there are many incommensurable degrees of freedom, and that they cannot be drawn up on a single scale of magnitude, however conceived. Moreover, in the case of societies, we are faced by such (logically absurd) questions as 'Would arrangement X increase the liberty of Mr. A more than it would that of Messrs. B, C, and D between them, added together?' The same difficulties arise in applying utilitarian criteria. Nevertheless, provided we do not demand precise measurement, we can give valid reasons for saying that the average subject of the King of Sweden is, on the whole, a good deal freer today than the average citizen of the Republic of Rumania. Total patterns of life must be compared directly as wholes, although the method by which we make the comparison, and the truth of the conclusions, is difficult or impossible to demonstrate. But the vagueness of the concepts, and the multiplicity of the criteria involved, is an attribute of the subject-matter itself, not of our imperfect methods of measurement, or incapacity for precise thought.

THE PHILOSOPHICAL
PROBLEM OF LIBERTY*

S. I. Benn and R. S. Peters

❖

Mill's argument rests on two principles that need analysis.

(a) All restraint, *qua* restraint, is an evil . . . leaving people to themselves is always better, *caeteris paribus*, than controlling them.[1]

(b) The sole end for which mankind are warranted, individually or collectively, in interfering with the liberty of action of any of their number, is self-protection. That the only purpose for which power can be rightfully exercised over any member of a civilized community, against his will, is to prevent harm to others. His own good, either physical or moral, is not a sufficient warrant.[2]

We must not interpret "self-protection" too strictly, however. Mill admits that it might be right to compel people to perform actions the neglect of which would be harmful.[3] It is a fair extension of the principle to allow compulsion where it can yield a positive advantage to others. The point of the "self-protection" principle is that it distinguishes two spheres of action; one, where the individual's conduct is likely to affect the interests of others, when interference is legitimate; the other, where conduct is wholly "self-regarding" and affects others for neither good nor ill, when interference would be illegitimate.

(A) "ALL RESTRAINT, QUA RESTRAINT, IS AN EVIL"

Mill offers no justification of the first principle; he treats it as self-evident. It is therefore beside the point that freedom may yield benefits; and similarly whatever benefits may arise from restraint, they

* Reprinted with permission of The Free Press from *The Principles of Political Thought* by S. I. Benn and R. S. Peters, pp. 257–262. Copyright © 1959 by George Allen & Unwin Ltd. First Free Press Paperbacks Edition, 1965.

[1] J. S. Mill, *On Liberty* (Everyman Edition), pp. 150–51.
[2] *Ibid.*, pp. 72–73.
[3] *Ibid.*, p. 74.

are purchased at a cost. Now a self-evident principle requires, by definition, no evidence or argument to support it; if it is possible for anyone who has rightly understood it to doubt it, it cannot be self-evident. At least one competent critic has found it possible to doubt Mill's assertion. J. D. Mabbott writes:

> I am still doubtful how far liberty is to be valued for itself and how far I am really counting on the . . . good effects of variety and experiment to which Mill so often appeals. For if liberty itself is what I value, it must have this high merit equally in the bad action and the good, and I cannot feel sure that, in a case where I knew I was doing wrong, it was at least one good element in the situation that no one tried to stop me.[4]

There is something curiously paradoxical about this which derives, in our view, from the language employed. Calling freedom to act "one good element in the situation," Mabbott treats it as if it were an ingredient in a composite whole, as one might say: "Though the cocktail was largely made up of vitriol and spirits of salt, the lemon juice was wholesome enough." But freedom to act is not a constituent of a situation separable from the thing done, and therefore capable of possessing distinct value. What is implied by Mill's principle is not that there is some value in the worst action if it is done freely, but that the onus of justification must always rest on the would-be restrainer, and not upon the person restrained. It is not that freedom of action is necessarily valuable in itself, but that there is always an initial presumption in its favour that must be overcome. And this is an accurate account of the way we carry on discussion in these matters. A writ of *Habeas Corpus* invites a gaoler to show good cause why his prisoner should not be released; the onus does not rest on the prisoner to make out a case for liberty. Similarly, in moral terms, if we find one man interfering with another's actions, and if we know nothing to start with about either, we should expect an explanation from the interfering one, not an account from the victim of why he should not be interfered with.

The presumption in favour of liberty is thus closely analogous to the presumption in favour of equality.[5] And the reason for it is the same, namely, that it is implied in the definition of a *moral* justification. Morality, we have observed, entails treating others as ends, never solely as means, or instruments. We do not ask a carpenter to justify using his

[4] *The State and the Citizen* (1948), p. 62.
[5] Cf. the discussion of equality in Chapter 5 of *The Principles of Political Thought*.

plane simply as a tool, nor a biologist to justify the detention of an amoeba on a slide. But we do object to treating men in this way; and if the only reason that can be given for constraint of one man by another is "I want to," the one is treating the other as a tool. Between the amoeba and the man there is an area of uncertainty. Many people today would feel it reasonable to ask a man to justify chaining up a dog; on the other hand, Aristotle was happy to defend slavery on the ground that some men were fit only to be the tools of others. To ask for a justification for a man's exercising a constraint upon another creature, is to recognize a moral relationship between them. One of the most important changes in moral attitudes since Aristotle's day has been the progressive extension of the class of beings that we treat as moral persons, so that now we not only include all human beings but, with some inconsistencies, the higher animals too.

The maxim "All restraint, *qua* restraint, is an evil" appears, on this analysis, as a way of saying that any restraint of a being who is a fitting subject of moral judgments, must be justified in moral terms. And this is logically entailed by the criteria defining the sphere of moral discourse. Consequently, it is a purely formal, or procedural maxim. It indicates where the responsibility for justification lies: it does not help us to decide whether a justification is adequate.

(B) THE "SELF-PROTECTION" PRINCIPLE

This problem, then, remains. Mill's "self-protection" principle is offered as a minimal answer, i.e. that any interference with purely self-regarding acts *cannot* be justified (which does not mean that all other interferences can). And this though the act in question may be morally wrong, like suicide or drug-taking; for the injury concerns no one but the doer.

This principle has been vigorously contested. Fitzjames Stephen, one of Mill's severest critics, roundly declares:

> There are acts of wickedness so gross and outrageous that, self-protection apart, they must be prevented as far as possible at any cost to the offender and punished, if they occur, with exemplary severity.[6]

The problem can be clarified by distinguishing between particular and general justifications.[7] As a criterion for interference in

---

[6] J. Fitzjames Stephen, *Liberty, Equality, Fraternity* (1873), p. 163.
[7] For further discussion of particular and general justification see Chapters 2 and 8 of *The Principles of Political Thought*.

particular cases, Mill's principle would be clearly at fault; where there is a rule, legal or moral, requiring or permitting interference with conduct of a given kind, it is not necessary to show that any particular instance of it is harmful to others, and we depart from the strict letter of the rule only in the exceptional case where it would tend to defeat its spirit.[8] The utilitarian consideration of "protection" arises only when the rule itself is in question.

In considering whether a rule is justified, we have to ask whether the over-all consequences would be bad if the type of conduct it prohibited became general. The sexual relations of A and B might be regarded, in a sense, as entirely their own business, if neither had marital or family ties. Yet there might be good grounds for banning relations of that type if the consequences to society generally would be bad, were they to be widely practised. Promiscuity or homosexuality could in many cases be defended as affecting no one but the parties taking part; but were the pressures of law and opinion relaxed, there might well be serious consequences for family life and the social structure, which on the whole we wish to preserve.

We have argued that to justify conduct of a given sort, we must consider with impartiality the consequences that would follow for everyone affected were it accepted as a general rule. On this basis, the class of immoral actions that affect no one but the doer—the class that Mill seeks to protect from interference—cannot exist; for if, considered as general social practices, they still affected only the doers, they would not be immoral. The only objection that could be raised to such practices is that they frustrated the doer from doing other things that he very much wanted to do. They would then be imprudent. They could only be thought immoral if the activities so prevented promised benefits for people other than the doer.

We have been seeking an interpretation of Mill's principles that would side-step the objection of their critics; they emerge as re-statements of the criteria of "morality"[9] namely, that "morality" involves respect for persons, and the critical assessment of conduct in terms of the consequences for all concerned if it were adopted as a general social practice. Unimpeachable as these principles are as procedural or formal criteria for moral judgment, they cannot provide the substantive rules for interference and non-interference that Mill expected of them. The most they will do is to rule out certain reasons for interfer-

[8] Elsewhere Mill accepts this view of justification of the particular instance. But he does not make this distinction in the essay *On Liberty*.
[9] For further discussion of the criteria of "morality" see Chapter 2 of *The Principles of Political Thought*.

ence as morally insufficient. Thus it is not enough to say: "I forbid
your way of worship because I do not like it," since mere preference is
not a *moral* ground for action. Since many people want to interfere
with others simply on account of an unreasoned prejudice, the connection between freedom and the criteria of moral justification may be
well worth while pointing out. Similarly, it would not be a moral
reason for interference with religious worship, to say "Your way is
forbidden by Holy Scripture"; for it remains to be proved that any
manner of worship so unauthorized would be harmful if generally
adopted. An appeal to the authority of scripture may constitute a
religious, but not a moral reason for an action or judgment. The
distinction between moral and religious reasons has been of the first
importance in the development of religious toleration.

Nevertheless, Mill did not do what he set out to do, and the main
question remains unanswered: What actions, that admittedly affect
others and so are the proper subject of moral judgments, ought
nevertheless to remain uncontrolled either by governmental or social
pressure? What we have said so far does suggest that any restraint
must stand up to objections of the following types:

(i)   in the case of a particular application of restraint, that the act in
question infringes no rule;
(ii) in the case of a general application of restraint, by a rule,
    (1) that the object of the rule is bad;
    (2) that while the object of the rule is good, the means pro-
        posed cannot reasonably be expected to attain it;
    (3) that though the object is good, and the proposed means
        would secure it, it is not of sufficient importance to warrant
        the degree of restraint proposed.

These are still formal principles rather than guides for conduct.
And we cannot expect to get further than this so long as we continue
to speak simply of "freedom," without completing it with particular
references to the things that we are to be free, or not free, to do. For
in applying formal principles, we must supply all the substantive
details, the conduct proposed, the attendant circumstances, and an
evaluation of the object of the proposed restraint. So far as we have
gone, it has been impossible to produce any general theoretical principles that lead necessarily to the conclusion that the classic freedoms,
of speech, thought, worship, assembly, etc., ought not to be infringed.

A RE-READING OF MILL
ON LIBERTY*

J. C. Rees

I

My aim in this article is to discuss what Mill was trying to do in his essay *On Liberty*. Or, to put it more precisely, to consider whether the commonly accepted version of 'the very simple principle' asserted in the essay is a fair account of Mill's intentions. Before setting out what I take to be the traditional version and giving my reasons for questioning it, we ought to remind ourselves of the general purpose Mill had in publishing his work.

In his *Autobiography* Mill describes the essay as 'a philosophic text-book of a single truth . . . the importance, to man and society, of a large variety in types of character, and of giving full freedom to human nature to expand itself in innumerable and conflicting directions'.[1] The book deals with one of the recurring questions of politics but was written in circumstances which gave that question a new significance. For behind Mill's question—'What is the nature and extent of the power which society ought to exercise over the individual?'—was his anxiety lest the tendencies which he claimed to see at work in the civilized world would eventually extinguish spontaneity in all the important branches of human conduct. 'Society has now [the manuscript was completed in 1857] fairly got the better of individuality . . . in our times, from the highest class of society down to the lowest, every one lives as under the eye of a hostile and dreaded censorship.'[2] The essay had, therefore, the practical aim of helping to ward off the dangers which the trends of the age seemed to carry with them and, in particular, to counter 'the general tendency of things

* From "A Re-reading of Mill on Liberty" by J. C. Rees, in *Political Studies* (Oxford: The Clarendon Press, 1960), VIII, 113–129. Reprinted by permission.

[1] *Autobiography* (World's Classics edition, London: Oxford University Press, 1924), p. 215.

[2] *On Liberty* (Everyman edition, London: J. M. Dent and Sons, 1931), p. 119. Quotations are from this edition throughout.

throughout the world to render mediocrity the ascendant power among mankind'.[3] The work, Mill tells us, was conceived and written as a short essay in 1854.[4] In a letter to Harriet from Rome in January 1855 he wrote: 'On my way here cogitating thereon I came back to an idea we have talked about, and thought that the best thing to write and publish at present would be a volume on Liberty. So many things might be brought into it and nothing seems more to be needed—it is a growing need too, for opinion tends to encroach more and more on liberty, and almost all the projects of social reformers of these days are really liberticide—Comte's particularly so.'[5] But Mill's fears and anxieties go back long before this period. They were clearly expressed in an essay on 'Civilization' published in 1836 and there are definite signs that they were taking root in even earlier years.[6]

One of the tasks Mill set himself in *On Liberty* was to fix a limit 'to the legitimate interference of collective opinion with individual independence'.[7] This seemed to him to be at least as important as 'protection against political despotism', for the 'yoke of opinion in England is perhaps heavier, that of the law is lighter, than in most other countries of Europe'.[8] The preservation of individuality and variety of character was possible, he believed, if a principle were observed whereby every person was accorded an area of liberty in thought and action. His father and Bentham had argued the case for representative government, but its practical consequences, whether in the United States as revealed by de Tocqueville or experienced in England since the Reform Act, were in his view by no means wholly favourable to liberty.[9] And even more menacing than the now appar-

[3] *Op. cit.*, p. 123.
[4] *Autobiography*, p. 212.
[5] F. A. Hayek, *John Stuart Mill and Harriet Taylor* (London: Routledge and K. Paul, 1951), p. 216.
[6] The essay on 'Civilization' is reprinted in *Dissertations and Discussions*, Vol. i (London: J. W. Parlin, 1859). See also Mill's article on 'Genius' (1832), reprinted in Ruth Borchardt's edition of *Four Dialogues of Plato*, ed. Ruth Borchardt (London: Watts and Co., 1946); and my article in this journal, 'A Phase in the Development of Mill's Ideas on Liberty' (vol. vi, pp. 33–44).
[7] *Op. cit.*, p. 68.
[8] *Op. cit.*, pp. 71–72.
[9] Before the publication of the first part of Tocqueville's work in 1835 the American Unitarian preacher and writer William Ellery Channing had uttered warnings similar to Tocqueville's at a number of points. Channing's writings were known in England and there were reviews of some of them in the *Edinburgh Review* and the *Westminster Review* in 1829 and 1830. I argued in a previous article in this journal (Feb. 1958) that Mill was influenced by Channing's views. Apart from the 'Remarks on the Formation of Associations', which Mill certainly knew, there is the election sermon of 1830. The latter was reprinted in a two-

ent weaknesses of a system of government whose establishment was the great aim of the orthodox Utilitarians were the informal pressures of society that the coming of democracy tended to strengthen and make still more relentless. Progress and the attainment of the truth were, as Mill saw it, the work of a select few; and to promote and safeguard the conditions for the distinctive activity of this *élite* in face of the growing power of the mediocre mass was a result he hoped his essay would help to achieve. Yet to a number who have shared his aspirations the specific principle he offered has always seemed defective. Mill's attachment to liberty has been admired on all sides and the many eloquent and moving passages he dedicates to its virtues have been widely acclaimed as classic utterances on behalf of one of the most cherished of western ideals, but, it has been generally said, the principle he advances for its protection cannot do what is expected of it. My purpose here is to look again at that principle and to discuss whether it has been properly understood by its critics.

II

'The object of this Essay', says Mill, 'is to assert one very simple principle . . . that the sole end for which mankind are warranted, individually or collectively, in interfering with the liberty of action of any of their number is self-protection . . . to prevent harm to others. . . . His own good, either physical or moral, is not a sufficient warrant. . . . The only part of the conduct of any one, for which he is amenable to society, is that which concerns others. In the part which merely concerns himself, his independence is, of right, absolute.'[10]

---

volume edition of Channing's works published in Britain in 1835 (see vol. ii, pp. 255 ff.). One or two passages are worth quoting. 'The advantages of civilisation have their peril. In such a state of society, opinion and law impose salutary restraint, and produce general order and security. But the power of opinion grows into a despotism, which, more than all things, represses original and free thought, subverts individuality of character, reduces the community to a spiritless monotony, and chills the love of perfection' (p. 268). 'An espionage of bigotry may as effectually close our lips and chill our hearts, as an armed and hundred-eyed police' (p. 271). 'Our great error as a people, is, that we put an idolatrous trust in free institutions; as if these, by some major power, must secure our rights, however we enslave ourselves to evil passions. We need to learn that forms of liberty are not its essence; that whilst the letter of a free constitution is preserved, its spirit may be lost; that even its wisest provisions and most guarded powers may be made weapons of tyranny. In a country called free, a majority may become a faction, and a proscribed minority may be insulted, robbed, and oppressed. Under elective governments, a dominant party may become as truly a usurper, and as treasonably conspire against the state, as an individual who forces his way by arms to the throne' (p. 278).

[10] *Op. cit.*, pp. 72–73.

This passage appears in the first chapter of the essay. In the last chapter, where Mill offers some examples of how his principle might be applied in practical cases, he restates 'the two maxims which together form the entire doctrine of this Essay . . . first, that the individual is not accountable to society for his actions, in so far as these concern the interests of no person but himself. . . . Secondly, that for such actions as are prejudicial to the interests of others, the individual is accountable, and may be subjected either to social or to legal punishment, if society is of opinion that the one or the other is requisite for its protection.'[11]

A study of the comments on Mill's essay during the century since its publication shows that the principle just stated has been widely criticized because it appears to rest on the possibility of classifying human actions into two categories—actions which concern only the agent and actions that concern others besides the agent. The distinction between these two categories, it has been repeatedly argued, is impossible to sustain. As one of the critics has put it: 'The greater part of English history since his day has been a practical commentary on the fallacy of this distinction. No action, however intimate, is free from social consequences. No human being can say that what he is, still less what he does, affects no one but himself.'[12] The crucial point in this criticism is clearly the supposition that Mill's principle depends for its validity on there being some actions, including some important ones, which are free from social consequences, i.e. that they affect no one but the agent himself.[13] I shall argue that this assumption on the part of the critics is false and that it derives from a failure to observe the form of words which Mill often employs in the text and to take at its full value Mill's firm assertion that actions of the so-called 'self-regarding' variety may frequently affect, even harmfully, persons other than the agent. Before elaborating this claim I want to pass

12 Leading article in *The Times Literary Supplement*, 10 July 1948. Reprinted as part of a pamphlet, *Western Values*, published by *The Times*.

13 'Including some important ones' is necessary here in order to prevent the issue from being trivialized. When Mill's critics say that no action is free from social consequences they must be assumed to be ignoring many petty acts which are obviously free from social effects, or else they are mistaken in refusing to admit their existence. For example, if I shave in a well-lit room before a mirror that reflects the face with uniform clarity and I can, in these conditions, shave equally well no matter which side I begin to shave, then starting with the left or the right side is a matter which cannot be considered to have any effects on other persons. Hence it is of no concern to society how I, or anyone else, begins to shave each morning. The debate between Mill and his critics clearly does not hinge on trivial acts of this kind.

briefly in review the evidence for my contention that the traditional account of Mill's principle makes just this assumption about his classification of human actions.

I begin with a commonly made criticism, drawn from among the first reviews of *On Liberty*. There is no conduct whose impact is confined to the agent, said the *London Review* in 1859, because 'no moral quality is limited in its action to the sphere of its possessor's own history and doings . . . society has an interest, over and above that of mere self-defence, in the conduct of every one of its members.[14] Fourteen years later, Fitzjames Stephen, whose *Liberty, Equality, Fraternity* has set the pattern for much of the criticism directed against Mill up to the present time, asserted with characteristic vigour that 'the attempt to distinguish between self-regarding acts and acts which regard others, is like an attempt to distinguish between acts which happen in time and acts which happen in space. Every act happens at some time and in some place, and in like manner every act that we do either does or may affect both ourselves and others . . . the distinction is altogether fallacious and unfounded.'[15] Further, in defence of the attitude of a temperance reformer whom Mill had attacked in the *Liberty*, Stephen remarks: 'It is surely a simple matter of fact that every human creature is deeply interested not only in the conduct, but in the thoughts, feelings, and opinions of millions of persons who stand in no other assignable relation to him than that of being his fellow-creatures. . . . A man would no more be a man if he was alone in the world than a hand would be a hand without the rest of the body.'[16] The view of human relations expressed in this last passage was, of course, shared by the Oxford Idealists and we should expect from them too a decided lack of sympathy with Mill's principle. Thus Ritchie considers the conception of the individual implied in Mill's doctrine to be abstract and negative, for the individual finds his true self 'not in distinction and separation from others, but in community with them'. 'We may very well doubt', he continues, 'whether any acts, nay, even thoughts, of the individual can, in the strictest sense, be merely self-regarding, and so matter of indifference to other individuals. . . . The more we learn of human society, the more we discover that there are no absolute divisions, but that every atom influences and is influenced by every other. It may be very well inexpedient to meddle

[14] Vol. xiii, p. 274.
[15] P. x, preface to the 2nd edition, 1874.
[16] P. 128 (1st edition, 1873). Mill's remarks appear on pp. 145–146 of *On Liberty*.

with particular acts, or it may be practically impossible to do so; but
we can lay down no hard and fast line, separating self-regarding acts
from acts which affect others.'[17] And Bosanquet: '. . . every act of
mine affects both myself and others. . . . It may safely be said that no
demarcation between self-regarding and other-regarding action can
possibly hold good.'[18]

Closer to our own day, MacIver in his *Modern State* remarks of
Mill's principle: 'This statement has a form which suggests that the full
significance of the interdependence of social beings is hardly realized
by Mill . . . he thinks of man as in certain categories social, but in
others wholly "individual". But if we realize that the nature of man is a
unity, that in every aspect he is a social being at the same time that he
is also autonomous and self-legislating, so that his sociality and his
individuality cannot belong to two different spheres . . . we can no
longer be content with an abstract doctrine of liberty.'[19] In a similar
vein Sir Ernest Barker says that Mill's assumption of the existence of
two different spheres of conduct is open to the criticism that Mill
separates the inseparable. 'The conduct of any man', maintains Sir
Ernest, 'is a single whole: there can be nothing in it that concerns
himself only, and does not concern other men: whatever he is, and
whatever he does, affects others and therefore concerns them.'[20]
Finally, to conclude with a quotation from one of the best studies of
Mill's philosophy that has appeared in recent decades, here is the view
of Professor R. P. Anschutz. He is commenting on Mill's principle of
self-protection ('the argument for insulation' as Anschutz calls it) and
says: 'It is a completely untenable as well as a completely impracticable
doctrine. It is quite impossible to distinguish between that part of a
person's behaviour which affects himself and that part which also

[17] D. G. Ritchie, *The Principles of State Interference* (London: S. Son-
nenschein and Co., 1891), pp. 96–98.

[18] Bosanquet, *Philosophical Theory of the State* (New York: Macmillan
and Co., Ltd., 1920), p. 60. Writing about the same time, Frederic Harrison
(*Tennyson, Ruskin, Mill*, London: Macmillan and Co., Ltd., 1899) states: 'The
attempt to distinguish between conduct which concerns oneself, and conduct that
may remotely concern others, is quite fallacious. No distinction can be drawn, for
human acts are organically inseparable' (p. 300). See also F. C. Montague's *The
Limits of Individual Liberty* (London: Revingtons, 1885), pp. 185–188: Mill's
distinction, says Montague, is an offshoot of the doctrine of the social contract
and 'is impossible to those who look upon man as receiving from society his whole
character and his whole endowment, and as reacting upon society at every
moment of his life.'

[19] Pp. 457–459.

[20] Ernest Barker, *Principles of Social and Political Theory* (Oxford: The
Clarendon Press, 1951), p. 217.

affects others; and there is nothing to be gained by attempting to make the distinction.'[21]

This, then, is the case which has been built up against Mill over the last hundred years. The essential point in the criticism is, as I have said, that Mill wrongly assumes some human actions to be free of social consequences. But if we look carefully at the two passages quoted above (pp. 89–90), where Mill is explicitly stating his principle, it will be noticed that, although in the first case he writes of conduct which 'merely concerns' the agent and of conduct which 'concerns others', he introduces the word 'interests' in the second passage. He says that the individual is to be held accountable only for those actions which 'are prejudicial to the *interests* of others'.[22] Elsewhere in the essay both types of phrase appear, with a number of variations within each type. Thus we find on the one hand: 'what only regards himself', 'conduct which affects only himself', 'which concerns only himself', 'things wherein the individual alone is concerned'; and on the other: 'concern the interests of others', 'affects the interests of no one but himself', 'affect the interests of others', 'damage to the interests of others'. Traditional commentary has assumed that all these expressions were intended to convey the same meaning and that Mill's distinction was simply between actions which affect no one but the agent and actions which affect others. My case in this article is that we ought not to gloss over these different modes of expression, that there is an important difference between just 'affecting others' and 'affecting the interests of others', and that there are passages in the essay which lend support to the view that Mill was thinking of 'interests' and not merely 'effects'. As a first step I wish to support my claim that there is a significant difference between saying, on the one hand, that an action affects another person and, on the other, that it affects his interests.

It seems to me quite clear that a person may be affected by another's behaviour without his interests being affected. For example, when we speak of a man's equilibrium not being affected in trying circumstances we are not thinking of his interests. Indeed a man's interests may well be seriously injured without his equilibrium being affected to any marked degree. And even if it were, there would be two things affected, not one. Similarly, if we heard of someone's outlook on life being fundamentally affected by an event such as a religious experience we should not have to conclude that his interests had likewise been affected. True, a religious convert has an interest in

21 *The Philosophy of J. S. Mill* (1953), p. 48.
22 My italics.

religion that he did not have before, but we are not speaking of interests in that sense. My interests in literature can undergo a radical change without anything like business, professional, or property interests being affected to the slightest extent. To bring out the distinction I am trying to make between interests and effects, but with no pretence at offering a definitive account of the nature of interests, one might say that interests—and I do not wish to imply that they are necessarily legal—depend for their existence on social recognition and are closely connected with prevailing standards about the sort of behaviour a man can legitimately expect from others. A claim that something should be recognized as an interest is one we should require to be supported by reasons and one capable of being made the subject of discussion. On the other hand I could be very seriously affected by the action of another person merely because I had an extraordinarily sensitive nature and no claim to have others respect these tender spots would be recognized as amounting to an interest. How one is affected by a theatrical performance depends partly on one's tastes, but the interests of a businessman would be affected by a tax on business property no matter what his tastes or susceptibilities; just as the interests of a university are affected by a scheme to establish a research institute in the same area (in a common subject of course) whether the university authorities welcome the idea or not. Moreover, 'effects' is a concept applicable to plants and animals as well as human beings, but no one talks about the interests of plants. Crops are affected by fertilizers or drought in much the same way as a certain drug would have an effect on, say, chronic lassitude. And dogs are affected by thunder in the kind of way that I might be affected by the news that my favourite football team had been beaten in the cup-final. There are no interests necessarily at stake here, though drought could affect my interests as well as the crops, and gamblers stand to win or lose by a result that could also leave them dismayed. Apart from really trivial actions—which we can ignore in this context—it is probably true that what I do or am like affects other people.[23] Any principle which rested on the assumption that other people are not (or may not be) affected would be open to precisely the objections brought against Mill. But deciding whether interests are affected is another matter and a principle that seeks to limit social interference to cases where interests are involved cannot be attacked because it fails to recognize the truth that 'every atom influences and is influenced by every other' or to realize that 'the nature of man is a unity'.

[23] See n. 13.

It might be objected at this stage that Mill does not consistently adhere to the term 'interests' and that one is not entitled to assume from its appearance in some passages, coupled with the employment of such phrases as 'conduct which concerns only himself', that there is one unambiguous doctrine running through the entire essay. Our objector might well concede the distinction between a principle based on interests and one based on mere effects, but he feels we are not justified in attempting to produce a coherent theory when, from the variety of the terms used in the relevant passages, there is clearly not one there to extract. My answer to this objection, for the moment at least (whether one can find a single consistent principle running through the whole work I discuss below) is that if Mill is really trying to maintain two (possibly more) principles, and moves from one to the other at different points of the essay without really knowing what he is doing and hence with no warning to his readers of what he is about, then to recognize this fact is at least to notice something which commentators on Mill have, so far as I know, failed to discern in the past. But it need not necessarily follow that because Mill uses phrases like 'conduct which concerns only himself' along with 'conduct which affects the interests of no persons besides himself' this must be regarded as conclusive evidence of an unwitting affirmation of two distinct and potentially incompatible principles. For though the word 'concerns' has sometimes no more force than 'has reference to' or 'affects', with no implication that interests are being referred to or affected, it can also mean 'is of importance to' and could in some contexts carry with it the suggestion that interests are involved. Thus when Mill says that social control is permissible only in cases when one's conduct 'concerns others' we are not compelled to assume that he means actions which just have 'effects' on others. Hence it may well be that the ambiguity of the word 'concerns' is responsible for concealing a coherent theory based on 'interests' rather than 'effects' and that we can so interpret the passages where the term 'interests' is not specifically used as to yield a single consistent principle.

However that may be, it should be observed that there are statements in the essay suggesting that Mill was quite aware of the manner in which individuals are constantly affecting one another. And so forthright are they that one wonders how it ever came to be thought of Mill that he wished to declare a whole area of human behaviour 'self-regarding' because the actions so named had no 'effects' on others (as opposed to 'affecting their interests'). Thus in the fourth chapter of the essay Mill discusses a possible objection to his principle in these terms: 'How (it may be asked) can any part of the conduct of a member of society be a matter of indifference to the other members?

No person is an entirely isolated being; it is impossible for a person to do anything seriously or permanently hurtful to himself, without mischief reaching at least to his near connections, and often far beyond them. . . .'[24] And Mill concedes to this objection 'that the mischief which a person does to himself may *seriously affect,* both through their sympathies and their interests, those nearly connected with him and, in a minor degree, society at large'.[25] But he goes on to insist that only when conduct of this sort (i.e. conduct affecting others) violates 'a distinct and assignable obligation to any other person or persons' is 'the case taken out of the self-regarding class, and becomes amenable to moral disapprobation'.[26] A little farther on in the same chapter Mill speaks of a person preventing himself 'by conduct purely self-regarding, from the performance of some definite duty incumbent on him to the public' and thus being guilty of a social offence, but where the conduct 'neither violates any specific duty to the public, nor occasions perceptible hurt to any assignable individual except himself, the inconvenience is one which society can afford to bear, for the sake of the greater good of human freedom'.[27] It is surely obvious that Mill would be contradicting himself here in the most flagrant manner if we were to interpret 'purely self-regarding' to mean those actions which have no impact (i.e. no 'effects') on other members of society. And the case against this interpretation becomes even more conclusive if we consider Mill's remarks in the opening chapter where he is elaborating the central principle of the essay. He writes: '. . . there is a sphere of action in which society, as distinguished from the individual, has if any, only an indirect interest; comprehending all that portion of a person's life and conduct which affects only himself . . . when I say only himself, I mean directly, and in the first instance; for whatever affects himself, may affect others through himself . . .'.[28] Further, in the fourth chapter, Mill talks of the 'self-regarding deficiencies' which a person may manifest and which 'render him necessarily and properly a subject of distaste, or, in extreme cases, even of contempt'. For vices of this kind, he says, a man may 'suffer very severe penalties at the hands of others for faults which directly concern only himself'.[29] Here, then, is a clear affirmation that what he calls, perhaps mislead-

---

[24] *Op. cit.,* p. 136.
[25] *Op. cit.,* p. 137. (My italics.)
[26] *Op. cit.,* pp. 137–138.
[27] *Op. cit.,* p. 138.
[28] *Op. cit.,* p. 75.
[29] *Op. cit.,* p. 134.

ingly, 'self-regarding conduct' can have effects on others. Even to the extent that those affected can retaliate with *'very severe penalties'!*

Mill's critics, Fitzjames Stephen among them, have wondered how the division of human conduct into two spheres could be sustained if self-regarding actions might suffer severe penalties at the hands of others. Mill attempted to maintain the distinction, which is, of course, crucial for the viability of his principle, in these words: '. . . the inconveniences which are strictly inseparable from the unfavourable judgment of others, are the only ones to which a person should ever be subjected for that portion of his conduct and character which concerns his own good, but which does not affect the interests of others in their relations with him. Acts injurious to others require a totally different treatment . . . these are fit objects of moral reprobation, and, in grave cases, of moral retribution and punishment.'[30] And as if to meet the objections of the sceptical Stephen, who could not see how 'inconveniences strictly inseparable from the unfavourable judgment of others' could be differentiated from the 'moral retribution' to be visited when other people's interests were harmed, Mill went on to show why this distinction was not merely nominal, in his eyes at least. In the former case the offender incurs a loss of consideration by reason of his imprudence or lack of dignity, whereas in the latter reprobation is due to him 'for an offence against the rights of others'.[31] And, claims Mill, people will react differently if the conduct of which they disapprove is such that they think that they have a right to control the agent. Whether Mill makes his point or not I do not wish to discuss further, but the words 'for an offence against the *rights* of others' raise a very important question and seem to introduce a new element into the principle. Nor is this the sole occasion when 'rights' are mentioned.[32] In the same chapter from which I have just been quoting, specifically devoted to discussing 'the limits to the authority of society over the individual', and therefore concerned to elaborate and give more detailed consideration to the principle mentioned and briefly treated in the opening chapter—it is in this fourth chapter that we should, I think, look for pointers to Mill's intentions—Mill attempts to demarcate the area of conduct for which we are to be made responsible to society. 'This conduct', he says, 'consists in not injuring the interests of one another; or rather certain interests which, either by express legal provision or by tacit understanding, ought to be con-

[30] *Op. cit.*, p. 135.
[31] *Op. cit.*, p. 136.
[32] See also *op. cit.*, pp. 120 and 135. (My italics.)

sidered as *rights*.'³³ Nor is this the complete extent of social control, for conduct may harm others 'without going to the length of violating any of their *constituted rights*'. In those cases punishment is inflicted by opinion rather than the law. Then, to sum up, Mill adds: 'As soon as any part of a person's conduct affects prejudicially the interests of others, society has jurisdiction over it', but no such question can arise 'when a person's conduct affects the interests of no persons besides himself . . .'.³⁴

The paragraph from which these extracts have been taken, coming as it does at a crucial stage in Mill's argument, is of some significance for the interpretation of his leading principle. It serves, incidentally, as further proof of my claim that it is 'interests' rather than 'effects' with which Mill is concerned. But its main significance for us at this stage is the appearance in it of the term 'rights' and the relationship Mill seems to suppose that term to have to the idea of 'interests'. From Mill's wording it is certain that the rights he has in mind are legal rights ('constituted rights'), for he envisages the law, rather than opinion, protecting some interests and these interests are then to be considered as rights. Other interests will not receive legal protection, though Mill does not exclude the possibility that these might be regarded as rights, though not legal ('constituted') rights. Certainly Mill is not saying that rights and interests are the same things, synonymous terms (and of course they are not), but he does seem to imply that they are very closely related to each other. It would be consistent with what he says here to suppose that when a person can be thought to have interests he is thereby possessed of a right, though not necessarily a right to the unqualified protection of his interests; perhaps only a right to have his interests taken into account. Moreover, by linking interests to rights in this way Mill leaves us with no excuse for confusing the notions of 'interests' and 'effects,' which must now be seen as belonging to quite different categories. It may be true that because of the element of vagueness attaching to rights and interests (i.e. as to what a man may legitimately, I do not mean *legally*, account his rights or interests) the concepts would be much more difficult to operate as part of a principle of liberty than the relatively simple notion of effects, but that ought not to blind us to the difference it makes to a principle to have the one rather than the other type of concept as a component.

---

³³ *Op. cit.*, p. 132. (My italics.)
³⁴ *Op. cit.*, p. 132. (My italics.)

III

The case I have been trying to make out is that Mill's principle of self-protection rests on a division of conduct into actions which either do or do not affect the interests of other persons rather than on what has generally been supposed to have been the division, namely, into conduct having or not having effects on others. This interpretation does not rely on the evidence of only one or two isolated passages where the word 'interests' appears. In fact the word appears at least fifteen times in the course of the essay and some of the passages where it is used are of the greatest importance in assessing Mill's intentions.[35] Furthermore, there is also the evidence I have already cited which shows how freely Mill admitted that what have commonly been thought of as literally self-regarding actions did have their effects on other persons. But having said that, I would be seriously misleading the reader if I failed to mention a number of difficulties which stand in the way of this interpretation or at least suggest that Mill was not always clear in his own mind as to what he wanted to say. The first difficulty arises out of a passage previously quoted in another context: '. . . there is a sphere of action in which society, as distinguished from the individual, has, if any, only an indirect interest; comprehending all that portion of a person's life and conduct which affects only himself. . . . When I say only himself, I mean *directly, and in the first instance;* for whatever affects himself, may affect others through himself. . . .'[36] And we find phrases similar to the one italicized here in other parts of the essay; for example, 'things which do not *primarily* concern others' and 'the part of life in which it is *chiefly* the individual that is interested . . . [as opposed to] the part which *chiefly* interests society'.[37] This seems to me a difficulty because if we are to take this passage seriously (and the repetition of like phrases elsewhere suggests it is not merely a case of careless writing) we should, on the account I have been giving, have to say that when Mill writes here of 'conduct which affects only himself' he means to say 'conduct which affects only his own interests'.[38] Further, since what affects my interests may also

---

[35] I have found the word on the following pages: 74 (twice), 75, 120, 132 (four times), 135, 138, 142, 149 (twice), and 150 (twice).

[36] *Op. cit.,* p. 75. (My italics.)

[37] *Op. cit.,* pp. 115 and 132. It should be noted, however, that 'primarily' and 'chiefly' are not equivalent to 'directly' or 'in the first instance'.

[38] In the first draft of this article the words 'to say' did not appear. I have inserted them in response to a remark made by Mr. J. M. Brown in some very valuable comments he kindly sent me on the draft. Mr. Brown pointed out that to

affect the interests of others, we should have to allow that 'self-regarding' conduct could affect the interests of others, though not 'directly' or 'primarily'. Hence the distinction Mill was attempting to make in his use of the self-regarding and other-regarding categories would seem to resolve itself into a division between (i) actions which primarily affect the interests of the agent but may affect the interests of others too, and (ii) actions which primarily affect the interests of others, though the agent's own interests may also be involved. It requires little imagination to foresee the immense complications that would be bound to arise in the application of such a formula. Nothing could be less appropriately described as a 'very simple principle'—Mill's own characterization in his opening chapter. Yet we should have to interpret these passages in some such manner or else admit, which is quite possible, that Mill falls occasionally into the language of 'effects', without realizing that he thereby allows a second principle to peep through from time to time while adhering mainly to a doctrine based on 'interests'.

IV

Assuming, then, that Mill's doctrine involves the idea of 'interests' rather than 'effects', is it, interpreted thus, a useful working principle of liberty in the way that the traditional version is patently not? The revised version would read something like this: 'Social control of individual actions ought to be exercised only in cases where the interests of others are either threatened or actually affected.'[39] But how to decide when interests are affected? What are interests? Is there any commonly accepted criterion, or set of criteria, of an interest? Mill's principle, as reformulated, must inevitably provoke questions like these and its value will obviously depend on the answers to be given to them. They cannot be fully treated here and all I shall attempt are some preliminary and tentative remarks.

As it is commonly used, the concept of 'interests' is an elusive one. There is no precise and generally acceptable definition. As Mr. Plamenatz observed in this journal, the idea of 'interest', compared with notions like 'right' or 'duty', is extremely vague.[40] But there are

---

allow 'conduct which affects only himself' to mean 'conduct which affects only his own interests' would undermine the distinction I have sought to make between these two types of statement.

[39] I am leaving out the complications connected with 'primarily', 'chiefly', and 'directly'.

[40] Vol. ii, no. 1 (Feb. 1954), p. 3.

many important concepts in our language which evade exact description and they remain none the less indispensable. Failure to bring the notion within the confines of a neat definition ought not to be a sufficient reason for rejecting out of hand a theory to which the concept is central. Moreover there are sociologists and jurists for whom the term occupies an important place in their theories. MacIver, for example, conceives human activity through the two concepts 'interest' and 'will'. There is, he says, 'no will without an interest and no interest apart from a will'. And by an interest he means 'some object which determines activity', though it is more than mere desire; it has 'a certain permanence and stability'.[41] Another definition of interest he offers is, 'the object of consciousness . . . anything, material or immaterial, factual or conceptual, to which we devote our attention'.[42] Roscoe Pound, too, employs the word with the same kind of wide meaning. For him an interest is a *de facto* claim and he draws up a comprehensive classification of interests which covers a vast field, ranging from individual claims to privacy to the social interest in free science and cultural progress. Among other writers the term is confined to certain kinds of consciousness or a particular class of attitudes such as, for example, those based on needs; and an appropriate list is provided of the bodily and spiritual needs which are to count for this purpose.[43] How are these uses of the word related to the normal sense of the term? Indeed, is it possible to identify an 'ordinary' use of the word? There would seem to be some grounds for saying that in a normal context an interest should not be construed as just a claim, far less any sort of claim. Rather it seems to be the condition in which a person's claim to, or title to, or share in something is recognized as valid by others, or at least is regarded as worthy of consideration. That is to say, there is an objective element about it which precludes any fanciful demand from being an interest. For interests are things we would generally look upon as deserving protection, to be prejudicially affected only by advantages likely to accrue in another direction. Certainly we feel that they ought not to be ignored even if there are compelling reasons for subordinating them to what we think are more important considerations. Interests, then, are not just arbitrary wishes, fleeting fancies, or capricious demands, though some of them may well

[41] R. M. MacIver, *Community*, 3rd edition (London: Macmillan and Co., Ltd., 1931), pp. 98–101.

[42] R. M. MacIver, *Society* (New York: Farrar and Rinehart, Inc., 1937), pp. 20–21.

[43] Alf Ross, *On Law and Justice* (London: Stevens, 1958), pp. 358–359.

have developed from forms to which these terms might have been
particularly apposite at the time.

Mill does not say much to indicate how he understood the notion
of interest, but there is nothing in the essay to suggest that he uses the
term in any exceptional manner. There is a passage, however, which
points to some of the problems inseparably connected with the idea of
interests. The secretary of an association formed to secure prohibition
had claimed a right to be protected from the consequences of the
liquor trade which, he argued, 'destroys my primary right of security,
by constantly creating and stimulating social disorder. . . . It impedes
my right to free moral and intellectual development, by surrounding
my path with dangers, and by weakening and demoralising society,
from which I have a right to claim mutual aid and intercourse.' Mill
repudiates with indignation such a sweeping claim, amounting, as he
saw it, to 'the absolute social right of every individual, that every other
individual shall act in every respect exactly as he ought' and conferring
on everyone 'a vested interest in each other's moral, intellectual, and
even physical perfection'.[44] Mill and the prohibitionist are disputing
what may legitimately be claimed as rights and what is to count as an
injury to a person's interests. According to the standards prevailing in
Mill's day, and certainly by those current in our own time, the secretary's claims appear ludicrously excessive and there would be no point
in taking his case seriously. But what is of importance is the very fact
of disagreement as to what a man may hold to be his interests. The
prohibitionist could have submitted the relatively modest claim that a
man's interests are prejudicially affected by the noisy behaviour of
groups of people gathering outside a public house adjoining, or close
to, his home. If the noise became such a nuisance as to lower the value
of the property it could not be denied that interests had been affected.
But apart from depreciation of value, has a man's interest been ad-
versely affected by the mere fact of disturbance of his privacy? He
could be the tenant of the house and suffer no personal pecuniary loss,
yet he might find the behaviour of the publican's clients extremely
annoying and might set a high monetary value on its cessation. Is it
part of a man's interests to be free from interference of this sort? From
the noise of the radio in his neighbour's flat or from the machines on
the airfield near his house? If we are going to say 'no' to the claim that
interests are affected by interference such as noise, as opposed to
monetary loss caused by noise, then this would seem to prevent Mill's
principle from operating in spheres in which he clearly wanted it to

44 *Op. cit.*, pp. 145–146.

work. But it is obvious that people can differ about what are to be
regarded as interests, since standards and values enter into what will be
recognized as interests (or what will *not* be recognized) at any given
time in a way that they do not in the case of 'effects'.[45] Consequently,
whether one takes a wide or narrow view of interests, the principle of
self-protection must necessarily harbour value-ingredients which will
inevitably render its use a controversial operation. That a drug affects a
certain disease is a strictly empirical matter. There are objective
procedures for tracing its 'effects'. It is true that there are also cases
when it would be a relatively simple matter to decide if my interests
have been affected: legal interests, for example. But there are also
occasions when, because standards differ, people will disagree about
what their interests are. And this is likely to make a principle based on
'interests' rather than 'effects' difficult to apply in many situations. For
not only is the concept 'interest' in itself vague: what are to count as
interests, even supposing there were a commonly accepted definition,
would be an open question in an indeterminate number of cases. Had
Mill formulated his principle in terms of rights rather than interests he
would have met the same difficulty precisely because what a man's
rights are is a question which can be reasonably answered in more than
one way.

　　Mill's principle raises yet another problem. Social interference, he
says, is justifiable only when the interests of others are affected but, he
adds, 'it must by no means be supposed, because damage, or probability
of damage, to the interests of others, can alone justify the interference
of society, that therefore it always does justify such interference'.[46]
Evidently the principle is not intended to absolve us from deciding
cases on their merits even when interests have actually been affected.
We should have to weigh up the advantages and disadvantages of social
interference on each occasion. As Mill puts it: '. . . the question
whether the general welfare will or will not be promoted by interfering with [another person's conduct], becomes open to discussion'.[47]
One of the examples he gives is the unsuccessful candidate in a
competitive examination.[48] Others have gained at his expense, but no

---

[45] And even if it came to be accepted that a man's interests were affected
by the noisy interruption of his privacy there is still the question of whether these
interests should be protected against other claims, such as, for example, freedom to
converse outside public houses, the demand for air travel, or the desire to listen to
music.

[46] *Op. cit.*, p. 150.

[47] *Op. cit.*, p. 132.

[48] *Op. cit.*, p. 150.

one would have it otherwise. A recent example would be the publicity given to statements warning of the harmful effects of heavy smoking. No one would wish to suppress information about the relation between smoking and lung cancer merely because it affected the interests of the tobacco firms. However, says Mill, in the case of conduct which affects no person's interests but one's own there can be no question of permitting social control and restraint: 'in all such cases, there should be perfect freedom, legal and social, to do the action and stand the consequences'.[49] So the principle provides us with a clear directive only when we can be sure that other people's interests are *not* involved; where interests *are* affected we are left with a margin of discretion and are advised to consider whether the general welfare is or is not likely to be promoted by interference in each particular instance. Hence the range of matters covered by the 'automatic' application of the rule is limited to those occasions on which it can be said that no one's interests have been injured. And it seems to be assumed that the question of interests being injured or not is one that can be readily determined.

It would be uncharitable to reject Mill's principle out of hand merely because it fails to provide an automatic and definite solution in an extensive range of cases (i.e. actions which *do* affect the interests of others). For how many of the principles we constantly wield in everyday life supply us with quick and certain answers? From Mill's point of view the important thing was to check the growing tendency to interfere in cases where intervention should be totally banned and for this purpose what had to be done was to demarcate the area of non-intervention from that in which a prima facie right to control could only be overridden by an appeal to the 'general welfare'. We have seen that with all its indefiniteness Mill's principle is emphatic on one point, namely, that when the interests of others have *not* been affected society should not intervene. But even here a serious doubt emerges. Are there not some actions we should want to control or prohibit which do not seem to injure the interests of others? Take the case of obscenity. It may be that some acts and some kinds of publications which the present law in the United Kingdom prohibits would be permitted in a more enlightened society, but there are certainly many which are, and ought to continue to be, prevented. Mill, too, seems to take this view. He refers to 'offences against decency', acts which, when done publicly, violate good manners, and places them 'within the

---

[49] *Op. cit.*, p. 132.

category of offences against others' and therefore to be prohibited. But
he remarks that offences of this nature 'are only connected indirectly
with our subject'.[50] Why this should be so he does not explain and it is
difficult to see what reasons he could have for saying it. Perhaps he
realized that to prohibit offences against decency on the ground that
they caused harm to other people's interests would involve a dangerous
extension of the conception of 'interests'. For whose interests are
threatened or injured by the appearance of obscene publications (or
the sale of opium, to take an example from a related field)? The
interests of those who concern themselves with public morality? Or
the social interest in maintaining standards of public decency? But if
we are allowed to bring in considerations of this sort, how could Mill
have maintained his opposition to a prohibition on the eating of pork in
a predominantly Muslim country?[51] Measures against the dropping of
litter or the emission of black smoke from chimneys in specified areas
are taken in order to protect the *public interest*, not because they
affect the interests of particular persons. That Mill recognized the
claims of the general interest is clear enough from his discussion of the
case of the person who instigates or counsels others to do acts which if
done of one's own free and unaided will would be 'blameable' but not
subject to social penalties because 'the evil directly resulting falls
wholly on the agent'.[52] On the one hand, argues Mill, people must be
allowed 'to consult with one another . . . to exchange opinions, and
give and receive suggestions', but the question becomes 'doubtful only
when the instigator derives a personal benefit from his advice' and is
gainfully occupied in promoting 'what society and the State consider
to be an evil'; for we would then be faced with a class of persons
having an interest 'opposed to what is considered as the public weal'.
Mill has in mind such people as the pimp and the keeper of a gambling
house. He fails to come to a definite conclusion about the justifiability
of prohibiting these activities, remarking that 'there are arguments on
both sides'. What is interesting in Mill's discussion here is—apart from
the confirmation that his principle can yield no clear directive in
questions of this kind—his appeal to 'the public weal' as a factor we

---

[50] *Op. cit.*, p. 153.
[51] This is one of Mill's examples (pp. 141–142). 'There are few acts which
Christians and Europeans regard with more unaffected disgust than Mussulmans
regard this particular mode of satisfying hunger,' says Mill. He goes on to argue
that the only good reason for condemning an attempt to ban the eating of pork in
a country where the Mussulmans were a majority would be 'that with the personal tastes and self-regarding concerns of individuals the public has no business to
interfere.'
[52] *Op. cit.*, pp. 153–155.

have to take into account before deciding on the legitimacy of social control. Does he intend that we should classify actions as being harmful to the interests of others if it could be shown that they are contrary to 'the public weal'? We are thus led back to the problem of how widely (or narrowly) we are to construe the notion of interests. Are we to interpret interests so narrowly as to exclude the public interest or so widely as to involve consideration of the general interest and social morality? On the former interpretation we should find ourselves unable to prohibit activity we should want to prohibit; on the latter we should be able to prohibit actions that Mill would certainly wish to be left unrestrained. And if standards and values enter into what we conceive to be a man's interests even in a restricted sense of the term, *a fortiori* they will shape what we take the public interest to require.

POSTSCRIPT (1965)*

Although I pointed out[1] that Mill sometimes explains his principle in terms of the violation of a man's *rights* I now feel this ought to have received more attention. In a more extended treatment of the subject which I hope to publish within the next year or two I shall seek to improve the analysis given in this article. For the time being I must restrict myself to showing the relevance of certain passages in the *Utilitarianism* for the interpretation given here of *On Liberty*.

In chapter III of the *Liberty* Mill says that individuality should be encouraged 'within the limits imposed by the rights and interests of others.'[2] A man should not be allowed to develop his own capacities 'to the injury of others' or at the expense of 'the rights of others.'[3] I take him to be restating the principle set out in the opening chapter and elaborated in chapter IV, and it is worth noticing that here in chapter III, he describes the limits to freedom of action as being 'held to rigid rules of justice for the sake of others.' In chapter IV of the *Utilitarianism* he gives an account of the nature of justice and says that it involves 'a rule of conduct, and a sentiment which sanctions that rule . . . a desire that punishment may be suffered by those who infringe the rule.' There belongs to it too 'the conception of some definite person

---

* Added by the author. Originally published in this volume.
[1] pp. 97–98 above.
[2] p. 120. As in the preceding article, all page references are to the Everyman edition.
[3] p. 121.

who suffers by the infringement,' whose 'rights' are violated by it.[4] Thus, Mill argues, essential elements in the idea of injustice are a person having a right and the infringement of that right. In this connection Mill speaks of 'some assignable person who is wronged' and this kind of language is reminiscent of a passage in the *Liberty* where he seeks to identify the line of demarcation between the areas of freedom and social control by describing self-regarding actions as 'conduct which neither violates any specific duty to the public, nor occasions perceptible hurt to any assignable individual except himself.'[5]

A man has a right, says Mill, when 'he has a valid claim on society to protect him in the possession of it, either by force of law, or by that of education and opinion;' it is 'something which society ought to defend him in the possession of.' And when there takes place 'a hurt to some assignable person,' together with a demand for punishment, we speak of a violation of a right.[6]

Are we entitled to assume that these and other similar remarks in the *Utilitarianism* are relevant to interpreting Mill's doctrine of liberty? I suggest that we are. Of the several passages which could be quoted in support the following is perhaps sufficient in itself: '. . . the moralities which protect every individual from being harmed by others, either directly or by being hindered in his freedom of pursuing his own good, are at once those which he himself has most at heart . . . (and) it is these moralities, primarily, which compose the obligations of justice.'[7]

I conclude therefore that there is much in chapter IV of *Utilitarianism* to support the kind of interpretation I offered in my article. It is true, however, that the emphasis in *Utilitarianism* is on 'rights' rather than 'interests' but I do not believe that this requires a substantial revision of my argument. I have already remarked that Mill talks of 'rights' in the *Liberty* and not, I would stress, in a casual way. 'Rights' is the term used in the passage quoted above from the essay,[8] and that passage has obvious points of contact with what Mill says about justice in *Utilitarianism*. Whether a viable doctrine can be built on the notion of rights is another question and is too large and complicated a problem to be discussed in this note.

[4] p. 49.
[5] p. 138.
[6] pp. 49–50.
[7] p. 56.
[8] p. 121.

DUTIES TO ONESELF*

Marcus George Singer

This discussion of prudence leads naturally to the question whether there are any duties to oneself. Many have thought so. One of the commonest divisions of duties is that based on the distinction between those that one has "to oneself" and those that one has "to others." Thus it is often said that it is a duty that one owes to oneself to preserve one's own life or develop one's talents or preserve one's self-respect. Consequently it is often held that suicide and sloth are morally wrong, on the ground that they violate one's duty to oneself. Few, perhaps, would go so far as Kant in claiming that "Our duties towards ourselves are of primary importance and should have pride of place . . . the prior condition of our duty to others is our duty to ourselves. . . ."[1] Yet many would agree that the distinction is both genuine and important, and it seems well embedded both in traditional moral philosophy and in ordinary moral thinking.

Nevertheless, it is actually impossible, as I shall argue, for there to be any duties to oneself, in any literal sense, for, if taken literally, the idea involves a contradiction. What are called "duties to oneself" are either not genuine moral duties at all, or, if they are, they are not duties to *oneself*. This leaves, of course, the question of what can be meant by the various expressions in which such "duties" are imputed, for I am certainly not arguing that such expressions are essentially meaningless or ought never to be used. My answer to this question will follow directly.

There are certain duties that we can quite clearly regard as being relative to persons, in the sense that we can speak of a duty *to someone* to do or forbear from doing certain acts. This is especially true of duties (or obligations) arising out of contracts or agreements, although

* From *Generalization in Ethics* by Marcus George Singer (New York: Alfred A. Knopf, Inc., 1961), pp. 311–318. Reprinted by permission.
[1] Kant, *Lectures on Ethics* (London: Methuen and Co., Ltd., 1930), pp. 117–118.

it is not restricted to such cases.[2] If I have promised you to do something, then I have a duty to you to do what I have promised, and you are the person to whom I have the obligation. If I have borrowed money from you, then I owe it to you and not to anyone else (unless you have assigned the debt to another), and I can be said to have a duty to you—namely, to pay back what I have borrowed—and I do not thereby have a duty to another. (This, of course, is what is said more simply and idiomatically in the statement that I owe you a certain sum of money.) Now, if I have a duty to you, then you have a right against or with respect to me. Thus, if I owe you a certain sum of money, then you have a right to receive and demand that money from me. In general, if *A* has a duty to *B*, then *B* has a right against or with respect to *A*.[3] But it follows from this that to have a *duty to oneself* would be to have a *right against oneself*, and this is surely nonsense. What could it mean to have a right or a claim against oneself? (Could one sue oneself in a court of law for return of the money one owes oneself?)

Yet my argument does not rest simply on the claim that it is nonsense to speak of a right against oneself, and that this is a necessary consequence of speaking of a duty to oneself. It is really more fundamental than this. It is essential to the nature of an obligation that no one can release himself from an obligation by not wishing to perform it or by deciding not to perform it, or, indeed, in any other way whatsoever. In other words, no one can release himself from an obligation, just as no one can release himself from a promise. To be

---

[2] Although for certain purposes such a distinction might usefully be made, I am not here distinguishing between duties and obligations. Cf. H. L. A. Hart, "Are There Any Natural Rights?" *The Philosophical Review*, vol. LXIV (April 1955), p. 179 note; also pp. 180–181.

[3] This statement by no means exhausts the subject of the relations between rights and duties. It is not intended to. The subject is complex, yet I cannot forbear mentioning that the question whether and how rights and duties are correlative has been clouded, not only by a failure to distinguish between different senses of "correlative," but also by a failure to distinguish different kinds of rights. There are, I think, at least three: (a) *action rights*, which are rights to do certain things, or to act in certain ways; (b) what may be called *receivatory* or *treatment rights*, which are rights to *receive* certain things, or *to be treated* in certain ways; and (c) *property rights*, which are rights *in* or *to* something. (These first two types of rights correspond, it may be observed, to what I before distinguished as the two sides of the generalization principle.) These different kinds of rights are related to each other in different ways, and they are also related in different ways to obligations, so that what holds of one may not hold for another. Cf., for an analogous distinction, Roscoe Pound, *An Introduction to the Philosophy of Law* (New Haven: Yale University Press, 1922), pp. 191–192.

sure, one can *break* the promise or the obligation. One can refuse to perform it. But this is not to release oneself. One can, however, *be released* from an obligation by the person to whom he has the obligation, just as one can be released from a promise by the person to whom he has made it. For one can give up his right against someone, or decide not to exercise it, and by this means release someone else from an obligation. But a duty to oneself, then, would be a duty from which one could release oneself at will, and this is self-contradictory. A "duty" from which one could release oneself at will is not, in any literal sense, a duty at all.

The situation is the same in the analogous case of a promise to oneself. Can one *promise* oneself to do something? Such language is frequently used. People say "I have promised myself to. . . ." (Note that the operative expression is in the past tense.) But a promise to oneself would be a promise from which one could release oneself at will, and thus not a genuine promise at all. The language here must be metaphorical. To say "I have promised myself to . . ." is to say "I have strongly resolved to. . . ." It is to express a settled determination to do the act in question, and in some cases the wish not to be dissuaded from it. Thus, though a "promise to oneself" is in some respects like a promise, it is not a genuine or in any literal sense a promise. For one can make a genuine promise without resolving or intending to do what one has promised, just as one can intend to do something without promising to do so. In the former case one would have made a false or lying promise, but one would still have made a promise. There is no analogue here with a "promise to oneself." To promise oneself to do something just *is* to be strongly resolved to do it, and if one were to change one's mind and not do what one intended one would not have broken any promise.

Consider also such expressions as "I owe it to myself to . . . " or "You owe it to yourself to . . ." Can one literally *owe* something to oneself, be in debt to oneself? Here again the language must be metaphorical. To say "I owe it to myself to . . ." is both a way of emphasizing one's *right* to do something and of expressing one's *determination* to do it. To tell someone that he owes it to himself, say, to take a vacation, is an emphatic way of asserting that he has a right to do it and of expressing one's belief that it would be decidedly imprudent for him not to. Thus it says no more than that he ought to, in the sense that it would be imprudent for him not to ("You need a vacation, you'd be foolish not to take one"), only it says it more forcefully. Similarly, no one can literally threaten or command or forcibly restrain himself, though such language can on occasion be psychologically or even socially useful.

These very same points apply to the notion of a duty to oneself. To say that someone has a duty (or owes it) to himself to do something is an emphatic way of asserting that he has a right to do it—that there are no moral considerations against it—and that it would be foolish or imprudent for him not to. It is, to be sure, to say that he ought to do the act in question, but only in the prudential sense of "ought." Thus, to suppose that one can actually have a moral duty to oneself, in any literal sense, is to confuse both a right to do something with a duty to do it, and an imprudent act with an immoral one.

If my argument is sound, then such expressions as I have considered cannot be given a literal interpretation. Yet they serve an interesting function in discourse. To say "I have promised myself to . . ." can often be a way of warding off objections to one's announced course of action and of enabling one to withstand them, as well as a way of *reinforcing* one's determination to do it. If we come to think that we have a duty to do something this can often save us from the onerous task of having to make up our minds what to do. To tell someone else that he owes it to himself, or has a duty to himself, to do something, can often be effective in persuading him to do it. For it can convey the idea that here is a case where both self-interest and duty combine in demanding a certain course of action. Apparently, then, what we have here is an appeal to self-interest disguised in the language of duty.

The argument that I have presented, against the idea that there are self-regarding duties, rests essentially on the following three propositions: (1) If A has a duty to B, then B has a right against A; (2) If B has a right against A, B can give it up and release A from the obligation; and (3) No one can release himself from an obligation. I must confess that I do not see how these propositions can rationally be denied. Yet one possible objection against the thesis I have presented might take the following form: In not every case can one be released from an obligation or duty. This may hold only where the duty arises out of a contractual relationship or some other voluntary undertakings. But not all duties arise out of contracts or promises or voluntary undertakings. Hence it may be that self-regarding duties are not duties of the sort from which one can be released.

My answer to this objection is that the relation I am presupposing as holding between rights and duties—proposition (1) above—is only asserted as holding for those duties or obligations that one can be said to have *to* someone. Consequently, if one could sensibly be said to have a duty to oneself, one would have a right against oneself that one could give up, thereby releasing oneself from the duty, which would contradict proposition (3), and be, in effect, self-contradictory. Now I can see no good reason for supposing that every duty must be a duty *to* someone. Many duties, to be sure, are thus relative to persons, are duties *to* some assignable individual or group, and this feature, as I have said, is characteristic of duties arising out of contracts or promises. But not all duties arise out of contracts or promises. Why then must all duties be supposed to have this characteristic? It is important here not to confuse the person *to whom* one is under an obligation with the person *regarding whom* one is under the obligation—that is, the person who stands to benefit by its performance—for they are not always one and the same.[4] *A* may have a duty *regarding C* without having a duty *to C*. Thus *A* may have a duty to *B* to pay *C* a certain sum of money, in which case it is *B*, and not *C*, who has the correlative right against *A*. It may be that it is this latter confusion that is responsible for the confusion about self-regarding duties. It may be that so-called "duties to oneself" are duties, or alleged duties, *regarding* oneself—in the sense that it is oneself who would be primarily or in the first instance affected by their performance or nonperformance—rather than duties *to* oneself. But this would not make this language any the less misleading, and I doubt whether the distinction can really be sustained along these lines.

What has just been said is sufficient to dispose of another possible objection to the argument I have been presenting, which may be derived from the arguments by which certain alleged duties are alleged to be duties. I have my doubts whether, to take the examples that are most usually given, it is a duty, in general, and apart from special circumstances, to preserve one's life or develop one's talents. But suppose that it is, and that it is morally wrong to commit suicide or waste one's talents. It would not at all follow that these are duties to oneself, merely because they would be duties with respect to oneself. Someone under military discipline may have the duty of keeping his shoes shined and his hair cut, and, in general, of maintaining a trim and

---

[4] Cf. Hart, *op. cit.*, p. 181: "It is important for the whole logic of rights that, while the person who stands to benefit by the performance of a duty is discovered by considering what will happen if the duty is not performed, the person who has a right (to whom performance is *owed* or *due*) is discovered by examining the transaction or antecedent situation or relations of the parties out of which the 'duty' arises." See also, on this distinction, W. D. Lamont, *The Principles of Moral Judgment* (Oxford: The Clarendon Press, 1946), pp. 80ff.

neat appearance. But these are not duties to himself, nor are they alleged to be. Kant's arguments to show the immorality of suicide and sloth (his first and third illustrations of the categorical imperative) have not the slightest tendency, even if sound, to show that these are breaches of one's duty to oneself. That there are duties to oneself is a supposition from which Kant starts, not a consequence of his argument. In effect, then, the question whether all duties are relative in the sense specified is not a matter of inordinate importance. A duty that cannot be said to be relative in this way to some specifically assignable individual or group still need not be supposed to be a duty to oneself. It can be regarded, if one so chooses, as a duty to one's society, or to mankind generally. (In that case, it would be what might be called a general duty, correlative to a general or "real" right, rather than a special duty [or obligation], correlative to a special or "personal" right.) Such, for example, is the case with the duty to pay taxes or to vote. Hence, if it really is a duty to preserve one's life, this can be regarded as a duty to mankind generally (if not to one's family). But this presupposes another classification of duties than the one mentioned at the outset.

In denying that there are duties to oneself, in any literal sense, I am not of course denying that there are what might be called self-regarding faults or vices. Similarly, in denying that one can literally promise oneself, owe anything to oneself, or threaten, command, or forcibly restrain oneself, I am not denying that one can harm oneself, or hurt oneself, defeat one's own purposes, or do what is detrimental to one's own best interest. Of course one can. A vice, after all, is a defect or an undesirable trait of character, a habit that it would be desirable not to have. Smoking, for example, is often said to be a vice. Suppose that it is. If it is, it is because, on the evidence available, it is likely to prove harmful to the agent and is thus a habit which, from the point of view of his own best interests, it would be desirable for him not to have. But it does not follow that it is a *moral* vice. In saying that a vice is an undesirable trait or habit, we must distinguish the interests with respect to which it is undesirable, the person or group of persons *for whom* it is undesirable. If it is harmful to the person who has it, then it is undesirable with respect to his interests, and thus it is undesirable from the point of view of prudence. It is, consequently, a self-regarding or prudential vice. On the other hand, if it is harmful to another or to society, then it is undesirable with respect to their interests, and is thus morally undesirable. It is, consequently, a moral vice. But not all vices, and so not all virtues, are moral ones, and it may be suspected that those who have crusaded, on moral grounds, against just such things as smoking, have been guilty of just this sort of obfuscation. On this matter, I think, Mill has said very nearly, though not quite, the last word:

Self-regarding faults . . . are not properly immoralities, and to whatever pitch they may be carried, do not constitute wickedness. They may be proofs of any amount of folly, or want of personal dignity and self-respect; but they are only a subject of moral reprobation when they involve a breach of duty to others, for whose sake the individual is bound to have care for himself. What are called duties to ourselves are not socially obligatory, unless circumstances render them at the same time duties to others. . . .[5]

[5] John Stuart Mill, *On Liberty* (Everyman's Library ed.; New York: E. P. Dutton and Company, 1910), chap. IV, par. 6, p. 135.

SUGGESTED FURTHER READINGS

SOME INEXPENSIVE EDITIONS OF "ON LIBERTY"

J. S. Mill. *On Liberty*, edited by Alburey Castell. New York: Appleton-Century-Crofts, Inc., 1947.

—————. *On Liberty*, edited by Russell Kirk. Chicago: Henry Regnery Co., 1955.

—————. *On Liberty*, edited by Currin V. Shields. New York: The Liberal Arts Press, 1956.

—————. *The Utilitarians*. Garden City, New York: Dolphin Books, 1961. This volume includes, in addition to *On Liberty*, Bentham's "Introduction to Principles of Morals and Legislation" and Mill's *Utilitarianism*.

—————. *The Philosophy of John Stuart Mill*, edited by Marshall Cohen. New York: Modern Library, 1961. Includes, in addition to *On Liberty*, *Utilitarianism*, "M. de Tocqueville on Democracy in America" the essays on Bentham and Coleridge, and others.

—————. *On Liberty, Representative Government, and Subjection of Women*, edited by Millicent Garrett Fawcett. London: Oxford University Press, 1960.

—————. *Essential Works of John Stuart Mill*, edited by Max Lerner. New York: Bantam Books, 1961. Contains, in addition to *On Liberty*, *Utilitarianism*, the *Autobiography*, and others.

—————. *Six Great Humanistic Essays of J. S. Mill*, edited by Albert William Levi. New York: Washington Square Press, 1963.

—————. *Utilitarianism, Liberty and Representative Government*, edited by A. D. Lindsay. New York: E. P. Dutton and Co., 1951.

—————. *On Liberty and Considerations on Representative Government*, edited by R. B. McCallum. Oxford: Basil Blackwell, 1948.

—————. *Utilitarianism, On Liberty, Essay on Bentham*, edited by Mary Warnock. Cleveland and New York: The World Publishing Co., 1962.

115

OTHER RELEVANT WRITINGS OF MILL

In addition to the works mentioned above as included with *On Liberty*, *Principles of Political Economy* contains relevant material. *Prefaces to Liberty* edited by Bernard Wishy (Boston: Beacon Press, 1959) reprints with *On Liberty* a number of pertinent articles and letters of Mill, including his long article "On Liberty of the Press."

GENERAL ACCOUNTS OF MILL'S LIFE AND PHILOSOPHY

R. P. Anschutz. *The Philosophy of J. S. Mill.* Oxford: The Clarendon Press, 1953.

Alexander Bain. *John Stuart Mill. A Criticism with Personal Recollections.* London: Longmans, Green and Co., 1882.

Karl Britton. *John Stuart Mill.* London: Penguin Books, Ltd., 1953.

F. A. Hayek. *John Stuart Mill and Harriet Taylor.* Chicago: University of Chicago Press, 1951.

Michael St. John Packe. *The Life of John Stuart Mill.* New York: The Macmillan Company, 1954. This is now the standard biography of Mill. It includes an extensive bibliography on Mill.

WRITINGS PRIMARILY CONCERNED WITH "ON LIBERTY"

For the extensive literature arising from Devlin's and Hart's recent dispute on the relation of law and morality, see the bibliography in Devlin. For further references on duties to oneself, see the bibliography in Singer's book. For independent discussion of the issues raised in *On Liberty*, often with reference to Mill, see the relevant writings of Bosanquet, Dewey, Green, Popper, and Russell, most of which are cited in one or another of the selections in this book.

Henry David Aiken. "Utilitarianism and Liberty: John Stuart Mill's Defense of Freedom," in *Reason and Conduct.* New York: Alfred A. Knopf, 1962.

Hannah Arendt. "Reflections on Little Rock," *Dissent*, VI, 1959. Miss Arendt argues, by way of distinctions similar to Mill's, that discrimination in the social area—schools, resort hotels, etc.—is legitimate.

Isaiah Berlin. *John Stuart Mill and the Ends of Life.* London: Council of Christians and Jews, 1961.

Patrick Devlin. *The Enforcement of Morals*. London: Oxford University Press, 1965. Contains, in addition to the original Maccabaean Lecture, a number of other essays on this topic, including "Mill on Liberty in Morals."

H. Gildin. "Mill's *On Liberty*" in *Ancients and Moderns: Essays on the Tradition of Political Philosophy in Honor of Leo Strauss*, edited by J. Cropsey. New York: Basic Books, 1964. Deploys some comments in Mill's *Logic* concerning freedom of discussion against *On Liberty*.

A. L. Harris. "John Stuart Mill: Servant of the East India Company," *Canadian Journal of Economics*, 30, 1964.

Harry A. Holloway. "Mill's Liberty, 1859–1959," *Ethics*, LXXI, 1960–61. A reply to the article by Levi reprinted in this book. The bibliography of this article is a useful starting point for anyone interested in discussions of Mill and Marx.

Richard Lichtman. "The Surface and Substance of Mill's Defense of Freedom," *Social Research*, XXX, 1963. Lichtman argues that Mill's real defense of liberty is in terms of self-realization.

H. J. McCloskey. "Mill's Liberalism," *Philosophical Quarterly*, XIII, 1963. McCloskey argues that Mill's position is not as liberal as it seems. There is a reply to McCloskey by A. Ryan in *Philosophical Quarterly*, XIV, 1964.

H. O. Pappe. *John Stuart Mill and the Harriet Taylor Myth*. Parkville, Victoria: Melbourne University Press, 1960. Useful in debunking the grandiose claims of Mill and some of his biographers concerning the extent of Mill's indebtedness to Harriet Taylor, claims made most strongly in connection with *On Liberty*.

H. O. Pappe. "Mill and Tocqueville," *Journal of the History of Ideas*, 25, April 1964. Downgrades Tocqueville's influences on Mill. Contains references to other material on the topic.

J. C. Rees. *Mill and His Early Critics*. Leicester: University College, 1956. This book contains criticisms made of *On Liberty* during Mill's lifetime and argues against regarding "Social Freedom," which argues for a position contrary to *On Liberty*, as a work of Mill.

Bertrand Russell. *John Stuart Mill, Lecture on a Master Mind*. Published for the British Academy by the Oxford University Press, 1955, from the *Proceedings of the British Academy*, XLI.

David Spitz. "Politics and the Realms of Being," *Dissent*, VI, 1959. A reply to Arendt by way of a criticism of Mill. These two articles would be useful to any student trying to work out the implications of Mill's essay in the area of civil rights.

J. W. Ward. "Mill, Marx, and Modern Individualism," *Virginia Quarterly Review*, XXXV, 1959.

E. G. West. "Liberty and Education: John Stuart Mill's Dilemma," *Philosophy*, XL, No. 152, April 1965.

Wolfenden Report. New York: Stern and Day, 1963.